The Essence of Brazilian Percussion and Drum Set

with **Rhythm Section Parts**

—— **Rhythms** ——
—— **Songstyles** ——
—— **Techniques** ——
—— **Applications** ——

By
Ed Uribe

The Essence of Brazilian Percussion and Drum Set

This book was desktop published and produced entirely by the author.
Audio CD recorded, mixed and produced at Big Daddy Productions, Englewood, NJ.
All instruments played by Ed Uribe.
All photographs by Gildas Bocle.

ISBN 0-7692-2024-X

About the Author

Ed Uribe is a graduate and faculty member of Berklee College of Music in Boston, Ma. He has also taught at Drummers Collective in New York City and appeared as a guest educator at numerous other schools. In addition to his role as an educator, Ed pursues an active free-lance career performing with major artists throughout the world. He has performed with Ray Barretto, Randy Brecker, Gary Burton, Michel Camilo, Paquito D'Rivera, George Coleman, Tania Maria, Donald Byrd, Dave Samuels, David Friedman, Claudio Roditi and The Toshiko Akiyoshi-Lew Tabakin Orchestra, among others.

As an artist endorser and clinician for Zildjian Cymbals, Pearl Drums, Afro Percussion, Vic Firth Sticks, KAT Inc., Korg Inc., Opcode Systems, Fishman Drum Triggers and Remo Products, Ed has appeared internationally at major jazz festivals and universities.

In the field of midi and electronic percussion, Ed performs solo concerts and clinics of his own compositions, and does programming and production work for various artists and studios. He is also a midi clinician/consultant and heads the electronic percussion and programming courses at Berklee College.

As an educational leader and in-demand player in the field of Latin percussion, Ed has developed and directs the Latin Percussion program of study for Berklee College and has written extensive educational material on this subject including his two books and videos on Brazilian and Afro-Cuban Percussion and Drum Set published by CPP/Belwin Inc.

Ed has lived in Brazil and also toured the country extensively both as a performer and a student of the music and culture. He also performed in Carnaval in 1983. Originally from San Francisco, Ed is currently based in New York.

Acknowledgments and Dedication

To be able to play music of any kind is a gift from a greater power. Although music is something that belongs to everyone, playing it is not something that everyone is able to do. It is sometimes easy to lose sight of what a privilege it is to be able to play and teach music as my livelihood. While a part of me believes that becoming a musician is not a matter of choice but a matter of inevitability, it is by no means an automatic occurrence to become one. It is both a lifetime and life-style commitment. It's just one you make at all costs. On the other hand, while you alone become a musician, you are bound in various ways to other individuals in order to exist with it. You need musicians to play with, an audience to play for, people to record you, and most importantly, teachers to learn from. While this learning process is lifelong and what a teacher is takes on many different forms as time goes on, one of your primary and most important relationships is with your teachers. A great teacher can make all the difference between having a healthy, secure vision of yourself in the music world, or feeling like you just can't crawl out from under the rock.

With these brief thoughts in mind I would most gratefully like to dedicate this book to Ed Valencia and John Rae. They are the type of teacher I am referring to. My gratitude also goes out to all the other teachers and musicians from whom I've learned this music, and played this music with.

Also thanks to Lennie D. at Zildjian, Scott, Bob and Richie at Pearl Drums, Vic Firth, and Lloyd McCauslin at REMO for providing the surdos. Many thanks to Tony, Mike, and the guys at O. DiBella Music for all the help with the instruments and for being a great music store. Thanks to Carlos Franzetti, Kip Reed and Mark Lampariello for their help with the rhythm section examples. At Berklee College, thanks to Dean Anderson, Larry Monroe and Dr. Warrick Carter for their support and also to Tony Marvuglio and David Mash for the technical assistance,

Thanks to Gerry and Ben James of Interworld Music for helping me get this project going. Special thanks to Sandy Feldstein for making this project possible, and last but certainly not least, my deepest thanks to my wife, Robin, for the long hours of editing the book and for her endless support of this inevitability of mine.

Table of Contents

Part I

Part II

About this Presentation

This material is a formal organization of musical styles that have survived and progressed from generation to generation through an oral tradition. It is not music that evolved from, or was taught through, formal education. This is the study of folklore. You are, in essence, learning a language—the language of Brazilian rhythms and songstyles. In learning any language, you study its components, the alphabet and its pronunciation, how to form words from those letters, how to make sentences and so on. The study of this material is the same. You will practice basic techniques and rhythms. These are the components. You'll then practice putting them together to play specific songstyles and to improvise in this idiom. In the serious study of a language, your goal is to speak, understand and be understood—to speak like a native. Your final goal in the study of a musical style should be the same. You should strive to play this music as if you had learned it in its purest, hand-me-down, oral tradition. Then you can truly feel you know how to play a style. The goal of this study is not to learn how to play a particular Samba or Baiaó beat, but to learn how to play Samba and Baiaó, along with the other styles presented. There is a big difference.

Part I deals exclusively with the percussion instruments. There is an individual section for each instrument that includes a description of the instrument and its traditional uses, the techniques of playing it and various rhythmic patterns for the more common styles. These include various styles of Samba, Baiaó, Choro, Frevo, Maracatu, Afoxé and others. Applications of these instruments and rhythms in styles such as jazz and funk are also included.

Part II addresses the drum set. Each rhythm is presented separately with some background information preceding the musical examples and exercises. Before the drum set examples of each style, there is a score of the basic percussion section and each instrument's respective rhythms. Before playing and as you practice the drum set parts, you should refer to these—and back to Part I—until you know at least the basic rhythms of each percussion part. Keep in mind that the drum set was not originally included in this music. To capture the essence of these styles in your set playing you must draw from what the percussion plays. The more you can do this, the more traditional you will sound.

There are short rhythm section examples included for you to see what the other instruments play in these styles. Notice how the rhythms of these instruments relate to the rhythms on the percussion and drum set. You can practice with these examples by playing them into a sequencer and cutting and pasting so you have a vamp of your liking to play along with. If you don't have a sequencer or piano chops you can ask a friend to record versions of these onto a tape machine and you can practice with the tape.

The audio recording includes examples from each section. Use it as your guide for how the rhythms should sound when you play them. The recording follows the order of the book.

The patterns included here are not merely exercises. The approach of this book is for you to learn the techniques of the percussion and drum set through learning the musical styles; thus really learning their role in this music. Therefore only material that can be, and actually is played in these styles is presented. While this compilation of material is by no means exhaustive, it is a reasonably thorough presentation of the role of these instruments in this genre. You should combine this material with listening to and studying as many recordings and live performances as possible. Even if you have no intention of actually performing this music, what you can gain by exposure to and assimilation of it is of tremendous value, especially to the drummer/percussionist.

Before delving into the musical examples, here is a very brief history of the development of this music and my connection to it.

Background Information

My coming to play Brazilian as well as other Latin styles of music developed from a purely drum set-oriented place. While growing up I heard a lot of music at home that I'll generically call Latin. I paid no particular attention to it. I liked some and disliked some. It wasn't until years later that I realized that I had been exposed to music from most of Latin America and much of Europe. On the streets I also heard different forms of Latin music, but none which I could identify in any specific way. At that time—the late sixties to mid-seventies— San Francisco had many musicians that were involved with integrating Latin styles with rock and funk styles. (Groups like Santana, Malo and Azteca come to mind.) This movement seemed much like the one that had taken place between Jazz and Latin in the 40's with people like Dizzy Gillespie and Chano Pozo. This music sounded different and I thought some was hip, but like most kids, was more in tune to the Funk, R & B and Rock sounds prevailing at the time. Aside from this, I had no other exposure or connection to this music. I mention this because in my involvement with performing and recording Latin-American musics, I've come across some attitudes and philosophies that say you cannot play these styles correctly—whatever that means—unless you are from a certain country and the like. This tends to sometimes discourage people from even trying to learn. It's true that to some degree you are a product of your culture and your time, but these styles can be learned and can be played. If you can groove you can learn any style. It's just like learning a language. You have to be around it and speak it enough and you'll start to sound like a native. There will always be people who will play styles better and more traditionally. Accept that as a given and try to learn from these people. In the end, your best lessons will be from people like this who are willing to show you. If someone discourages you just move on.

When I began taking drum lessons I was shown, among other things, Brazilian styles like Bossa Nova, Samba and Baião, and Afro-Cuban styles like the Cha-Cha and Mambo. Playing these rhythms was so different than any of the other stuff on the drums. They didn't feel like they were from the drum set and of course, I later found out they weren't. The syncopations in the rhythms felt so different and so good. I started to check out recordings and to go see this music played live. The music made me move my body in such a different way. I kept checking out more music and I kept asking to be shown more of these grooves and it hasn't stopped to this day. While at that time most of these rhythms were merely hip grooves on the drum set, it wasn't long before I got completely immersed in the different styles and percussion instruments. My first musical tour to Brazil was in 1982. I was to play there six weeks and return home. Instead I returned almost a year later. I've since had the good fortune to perform in Latin and South America extensively, and every time I go I inevitably come back amazed at some new rhythm or instrument I was exposed to.

In the course of exploring and performing this music I've discovered an unfortunate fact. Most Americans and many American musicians perceive everything south of the Texan border to be just plain *Latin*—one big generic category with a singular identity. Not only is this perception grossly imprecise, but for a musician it is unacceptable. It is important that you become aware of the vast differences that exist between the varied cultures in Latin America and the Caribbean, particularly in their music, and especially if you are a drummer/percussionist.

Most of the music of Latin America shares three common cultural elements: The African culture of the slaves brought there by the Europeans, the folklore of the native Indians, and the European traditions of whatever power dominated that particular region between the fifteenth and eighteenth centuries. Aside from these common threads, there are countless distinctions to be noted and countless musical styles to explore.

Following is a list of a few common musical styles from various Latin American and Caribbean countries:

- **Argentina:**   *Tango, Milonga, Zamba, Chacarera*
- **Uruguay:**   *Candombe, Zamba*
- **Columbia:**   *Cumbia, Bambuco*
- **Venezuela:**   *Joropo, Valse*
- **Ecuador:**   *Pasillo, Taquerari*
- **Chile:**   *Cueca*
- **Peru:**   *Guaino, Vals Peruano, La Marinera*
- **Andean Styles**   *Baguala, Carnavalito, Vidala*
- **Mexico:**   *Musica Ranchera, Mariachi, Mayan Marimba Styles and forms of Danzon, Joropo Mejicano*
- **Puerto Rico:**   *Bomba, Plena*
- **Dominican Republic:** *Merengue*
- **Trinidad:**   *Calypso, Soca*
- **Haiti:**   *Merengue, form of French Variation*
- **Jamaica:**   *Reggae*
- **Cuba:**   *Son, Mambo, Cha-cha, Guaguancó, Mozambique, Bembé, Abakwa, Guajira, Charanga, Rumba styles, Batá rhythms, Songo, Conga and Comparsa, Palo*

And finally the topic of this book:

- **Brazil:**   *Bossa Nova, Samba, Baiaó, Frevo, Maracatu, Chorinho, Capoeira, Candomble, Afoxé, Xote, Maxixe*

These are just a few of the many, and this is just one part of the world. Think of the wealth of rhythms and percussion instruments there are to explore. This should be important to you for two reasons. First, as a drummer/percussionist, learning the musical styles of these many cultures will greatly expand your rhythmic vocabulary and your playing no matter how you choose to adopt or apply them. Second, as a musician you have the opportunity to reach and influence large numbers of people. You can easily help educate people and spread the beauty of these musics.

Developments in Brazil

Since the beginning of time cultures have merged and formed new, or at the very least, integrated folklore. Unfortunately much of this merging wasn't a willful, cooperative effort between cultures. It was generally forced upon peoples by stronger, imperialist powers whose motives were certainly not to develop new cultural traditions. Many times this imposition of will has completely annihilated peoples, or has left cultures in conflicts that have lasted generations. The transferring of people from their homeland, as was done with West Africans made slaves in the fifteenth through seventeenth centuries by European powers, or the drawing of a geographic boundary through the land of a people existing intact, have forced cultures to acclimate to different homelands and the practices of unfamiliar peoples.

While the suffering caused by these integrations can hardly be seen as positive, there were seeds planted that gave birth to musical styles that have shaped the development and direction of music throughout the world.

When these forced mergings took place, generally a couple of things happened. The empowering culture enslaved and imposed its customs on the native people. If this was not possible they sometimes simply eliminated them. They then brought in other already enslaved people for labor purposes in the exploitation of what they now viewed as their new land. While the ruling powers were doing their best to reorient these people to their customs, and in many instances forbidding them to continue their own cultural practices, these groups attempted to continue their traditions in whatever way they could. With each ethnic group carrying on their own practices in a new and integrated land, the result was a tremendous blending of music, religion, languages and social customs.

In Brazil these events began taking place in 1500 when the Portuguese explorer Pedro Álvares Cabral landed in what is now the state of Bahia. There he found an indigenous population of countless tribes of Indians that had existed in this land for thousands of years. (History shows two to three million inhabitants, dating their migration towards these regions back 40,000 years.) In a very short time, these people were enslaved and many eliminated. The enslaved Indians did not provide the Portuguese with the labor force they needed to exploit the wealth of mineral and agricultural resources of this land. The next step brought the African slaves. From the early 1500's to the mid-1800's, approximately 3.5 million Africans survived the crossing to Brazil. (This is five to six times more than were brought to North America during this period of slavery.) Hence the merging of various tribes of native Indians, Africans—also of varied regions and tribes, though mostly from the northwestern parts of Africa—and the Portuguese, began.

Brazilian music evolved from these three cultures, Indian, African and Portuguese, but of the three the Indian influence is the least pronounced and the African the most. The minor role Indian music played in the evolution was due in part to the Jesuits who, upon their arrival in Brazil in the mid-1500's, set out to re-educate these people, teaching them to practice European customs and teaching them the "benefits" of Christianity; thus suppressing their cultural and religious practices. This re-education was part of the mission of the explorers in the new world. Although the Indians had a long-standing folklore, they tended to lose their cultural traditions in their diaspora and in their integration with the whites. The Indian population in Brazil is today roughly ten percent of what it was then.

For the Africans, music and drumming were an integral part of daily life. Their religious rituals also involved them extensively. These people brought and maintained their customs in a form more indigenous to their cultural roots. This is due to several reasons. First, the re-education the explorers were attempting with the native Indians was not done with the Africans. They were enslaved and their education was not in the program. The only effort made was to not allow them to practice their folkloric customs, but they were not as closely observed as the Indians and thus were able to continue some of their rituals. Second, throughout history, all European conquerors made an effort to keep their African slaves from practicing their customs (with the northern Protestant Europeans being the most oppressive). The Portuguese were no exception. but although they made efforts to suppress the religious practices of the Africans, they were more tolerant of the African cultural practices than their northern European counterparts. This may in part be due to the fact that the Iberian Peninsula had interaction with the North Africans—mostly in the form of wars and enslavement between the Moors and the Christians—that dates back to the twelfth century and were thus more accustomed to some integration. Furthermore, the Portuguese explorers—as well as the Spanish and French—were mostly male, versus the migration of entire families of English Protestant backgrounds to North America. Thus their tendency to integrate, even if only for propagation, was greater than that of the northern Europeans, who, having emigrated with their entire families, generally disdained any type of integration and went through great efforts to suppress the African culture. The southern European explorers and settlers, to some degree, had no choice but to mix and the melting pot began.

The Portuguese brought with them the European melodic and harmonic traditions. These included Spanish, French and some northern European influences. The elements of both sacred and secular music were present in their melodies, harmonies, polyphony in the vocal music, and certain verse-chorus and chant song structures. Certain percussion instruments such as bass drums and snare drums had some of their origin in military marches. All of these became integral parts of many Brazilian styles. The more folkloric elements included the tambourine—an extremely popular instrument in Portugal, the Basque regions of Spain and France, several other areas of northern Europe and regions of the middle-east. This gave way to the Brazilian Pandeiro, an instrument that has been developed to the point of true artistry by Brazilian percussionists. Stringed instruments brought by the Portuguese also influenced the development and use of the Cavaquinho—a small four-stringed guitar very common in samba music, as well as the six-string guitar in later styles. Last but certainly not least, the Portuguese brought their language. Brazilian Portuguese developed into a lyrical and sensual version of the language that lends itself to a captivating and alluring vocal music style. It also makes Brazil unique as the only non-Spanish speaking country in Latin America.

The Africans brought with them predominantly vocal and rhythmic elements as well as percussion instruments that served as the origin for many that are an integral part of Brazilian and Latin-American music today. Initially the Portuguese brought Africans from their colonies in Mozambique and Angola as well as the Congo. Later, as slave trading to the west increased, many were also brought from northwestern regions. Again, both sacred and secular influences are present in the African contributions. The call and response vocal styles and drumming of the Yoruba people—from present-day Nigerian regions—illustrates the influence of religious music and dance and is still very present in many northern Brazilian musical styles—particularly Candomble music. Duple meter with layering of triple meters from the African 6/8 traditions as well as the layering of various rhythms over an ostinato pulse are some rhythmic elements of African music that are very much the structural foundation of many Brazilian rhythms today. Many percussion instruments of African origin such as various shakers made of weaved baskets, instruments made from gourds such as shekerés, single headed, conga-like drums, some double-headed drums and scraper-type instruments gave way to the development of caxixi, afoxé, chocalos, atabaque, reco-reco, the berimbau and a wealth of other instruments used in Brazilian styles. African culture was most influential in the development of the styles of northern Brazil. It has survived more intact, and is more prevalent in this region than in any other in the country.

Indian influence, as mentioned before, was less apparent. Nonetheless, contributions in the area of flutes, certain vocal styles and certain percussion instruments such as rattles and shakers made from gourds and some weaved basket shakers can be traced to Indian roots. Although not as prevalent in the Brazilian musical styles that are presented in this text, Indian music is quite present in many western (Amazonian) regions of Brazil, as well as in many of the Andean regions such as those of Ecuador and Peru.

All of these cultural elements combined to form the basis of the musical styles which will be presented in this text. These styles were chosen because they are the most prevalent styles in Brazilian popular music and have had the largest effect on other music throughout the world. Its influence and integration into American styles of jazz, funk, R & B and other popular music is so great that it is almost essential that all musicians become familiar with them. It can safely be said that in the present day, Brazil—along with Cuba and American popular music—has had the greatest influence on popular music throughout the world. Brazil and Cuba—along with African music—have also had the greatest influence on all types of American music.

All of the songstyles of Brazil—the many Sambas, Baiaó, Frevo, Maracatu, Candomble, Maxixe, Chorinho, Coco and Afoxé—exhibit the aforementioned influences. This historical information is very general. It would be almost impossible to list all of the hundreds of musical styles of Brazil and present their precise origins and development, as many of them are even unknown. To present those that are known would require a multi-volume work and a lifetime of study. While I encourage you to research the different musical styles, as it is a fascinating study, the purpose of this presentation is to learn the most popular and influential of the rhythms, songstyles, percussion instruments and how to apply them to the drum set so, onward.

11

Map of Brazil and Related Regions

How to Learn and Practice this Material

How you should approach learning this material depends largely on your technical proficiency on the percussion instruments and drum set, and on whether you have any prior exposure to these styles. It should go without saying—but I'll say this anyway. You have to have your basics down before you can make this material sound right. Your basic hand and stick techniques, coordination, foot technique, reading, counting in various time signatures, and more than anything, your time. Without this you have nothing!

If you are primarily a drum set player, you should focus on learning the percussion instruments and rhythms first. As mentioned earlier, the more you can incorporate and draw from the percussion and traditional rhythms, the more you will play the style with an authentic sound. When you're actually playing, the choice becomes yours, but having this knowledge under your belt will enable you to play this way if you want or need to. If you are primarily a percussionist, then you may already know some or all of the material in the first part. You should review and then work on the drum set. If you don't have basic drum set skills, you may need to do some other technical studies since some of this material requires a pretty reasonable degree of hand–foot coordination and stick technique.

If you already play on an intermediate to advanced level, you should get familiar with this material from a more traditional perspective. Practice it, memorize the patterns and practice improvising with it. Get recordings—there is suggested listening throughout the text—and learn how this material works in the actual music. Your next order of priority should be to find playing situations where you can apply this material.

If you are more of a beginner or coming to this music for the first time, my advice is to get a good teacher to guide you. If you don't know how this material is supposed to sound, you need someone to hear you play and tell you if you're on the right track. It is also very important that you listen to recordings of these styles. The recording provided with this book should be your primary guide for how these examples should sound. Next listen to how these rhythms take place in actual recordings and live performance.

A few things to keep in mind: The music itself will almost always tell you what can and should be played. Hence variations, approaches and articulations—other than those in this book—will enter into the picture. In an improvisational idiom, other factors—particularly those of interplay between the musicians—will also dictate what to play. However, many situations will accommodate and may even require the types of rhythms presented here. Again, listen to the recording provided and as many recordings and live performances as you can, as well as find performance situations in which you can apply this material. Your actual playing and experimentation will be your best learning experience. When you do get an opportunity to play this music with people who really know it, keep your eyes and ears wide open. These will be your most valuable lessons. Pick their brains whenever the situation allows. When practicing this material think music, not exercises. What you're striving for primarily is a good authentic feel.

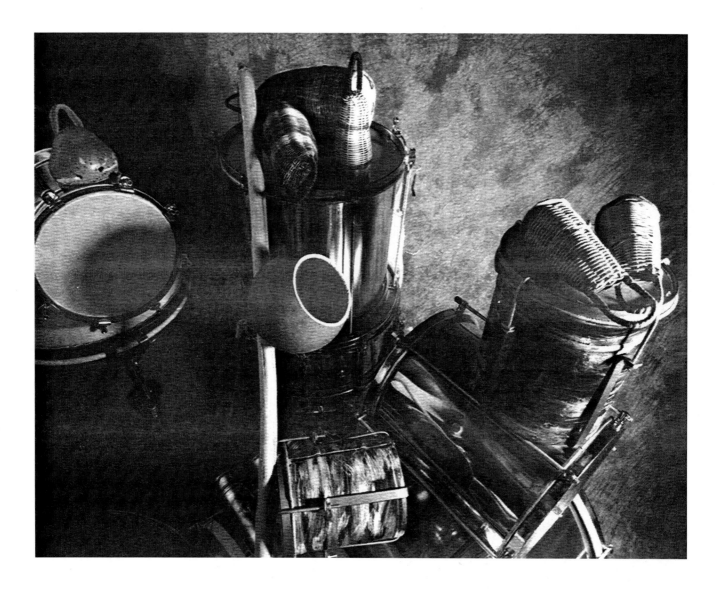

Part I

Brazilian Hand Percussion

——— **Rhythms** ———
——— **Songstyles** ———
——— **Techniques** ———
——— **Applications** ———

The Songstyles

Brazil, like all other countries in South America, the Caribbean and Africa, has a vast number and variety of songstyles, rhythms and instruments indigenous to its folklore. In spite of the many Brazilian styles, most would agree that three styles are most known, and have had the biggest influence on popular music throughout the world.

The first of these is the Samba and its derivative styles. Its derivations are mostly based on either the actual musical form or approach—such as in the samba cancaó or samba marcha, or on a particular region or neighborhood that the particular style emanated from—such as the samba de morro (refers to samba from the hills surrounding Rio). The second of these is the Bossa Nova. This rhythm and songstyle will be addressed in the second part of the book. The third is the Baiaó and its related styles from the northern regions of the country. The styles from the northern parts of the country most exhibit the African heritage and influence in Brazil's music. They are not necessarily specifically related to the Baiaó rhythm, but for our purposes will be presented under this general category of northern styles. Under these two broader topics of Samba and Baiaó, we'll examine the rhythms, songstyles, performing ensembles and related topics from which the musical examples in this book emanate.

Brazil's many musical forms can further be categorized as follows. (You can keep the following in mind if you are interested in further studies of this culture and its music.) The first category, secular/popular music, would include the many Samba styles, the Bossa Nova and the Baiaó. Also included would be the predecessors of these styles, the *Lundú, Maxixe, Jongo, Coco and the Batuque*—the style from which the Batucada developed. The second category, sacred/religious styles, would include the Candomble, the Afoxé and styles that are used for other Afro-Brazilian religions such as Catimbó, Umbanda and Xangô. This category of sacred styles would also have a sub-category of styles used for certain rituals that may or may not be religious but have roots in ritual practices, dance exhibitions, processional dances or call and response type singing in certain cultures. This group would include the Capoeira style, the Maracatú, Frevo and various Congadas. The Batuque could also be placed in this category. All of these song forms have also given way to many hybrid combinations mixing various Brazilian styles as well as mixing Brazilian styles with the music of other cultures.

Samba, Carnaval and the Escolas

A single technical definition could not accurately express what Samba truly is. Other than to say the obvious about it being the most popular Afro-Brazilian musical form in its country, and probably the most well-known throughout the world, everything else must be broken down into categorical and characteristic definitions—historical accounts, the musical and theoretical elements, the social aspects and finally the subjective definitions that don't always have to do with the actual musical form. To give an accurate historical account of the evolution of Samba is also difficult, as the actual origin is really unknown. There are quite a few theories though, and there are several elements that most seem to agree upon. The African roots of the Samba seem to be from the *round* or *circle* dances from *Angola*. These are known as *Congadas* in Brazil. The term and dance called *Semba*—from the Kimbundu tribe in Angola—is a dance featuring the *Umbigada*. *Umbiga* is the Portuguese word for navel. The umbigada was part of African dances like the *Batuque* in which one dancer would touch their navel against that of the other. This was sometimes the invitation to dance from one row of dancers to the other. Many African dance styles that featured this. Other African and Afro-Brazilian styles—the Lundú, Coco, Batuque and Jongo—also played a role in the evolution of Samba as they were brought south to Rio from the Bahian regions by slaves and former slaves emigrating from the poverty of the north to the more financially prospering capital in the late 1800's. Slavery was, at least officially, abolished in Brazil in 1888. This accounted for large numbers of Afro-Brazilians emigrating from the north. This can account for one theory that Samba has its roots in Bahia. While there are many more details and many variations to the general theories presented here, all agree that the real evolution and development of Samba took place in Rio, where it came to have a characteristic very distinct from other Afro-Brazilian songstyles.

In the early 1900's a small Africa came to exist in Rio due to the influx of African slaves from Bahia and other northern regions. An area in Rio called *Praça Onze* (Plaza Eleven) was one of the initial and primary gathering places of these new emigres. The music played during these gatherings planted the seeds for the style that would later become the Samba. These initial gatherings had an influx of many musical styles that had developed through the integration of the different African, European and Indian cultures. These gatherings and the music they generated began to spread throughout the *favelas* (poor neighborhoods) of Rio and Samba began developing. The new immigrants from the north continued their traditions of *Orixa* (African or Afro-Brazilian gods) worship, which almost always included music and dance, and continued making music and dance for their daily consumption. The gatherings for the worship of these *Orixas* took place in the homes of old Bahian matriarchs called *tias* (aunts). These tias successfully did a great deal to keep their African or Afro-Brazilian culture alive. They are honored today during *Carnaval* by the *Ala de Baianas* in the *Escola de Samba*.

Early musicians gathering in these *favelas* began to shape the Carioca Samba (urban Samba from Rio) of today from the influences of the still developing forms of the duple meter marcha, maxixe, tango, habanera, polka, and lundú, as well as other influences that resulted from all the European and African integration of the previous three centuries. Important musicians from this area include the composer/arrangers Pixinguinha and Sinhô, Joaó de Baiana, who is credited with introducing the pandeiro as a samba instrument, and Ernesto dos Santos, known as Donga, who co-composed the first official Samba, *Pelo Telefone* in 1917. The song was released by a group called Banda Odeon and spread rapidly due to the newest media of the time, radio.

Samba made further developments in an area called *Estácio*. These sambistas (samba innovators), as they came to be known, began making clearer distinctions between Samba and Marcha and Maxixe. Clearer musical characteristics evolved and began to define the early Samba. Some of these were duple meter with a heavier accent on the second beat—the *two* of the bar—compound, layered and syncopated rhythms, and rhythmic structure in the percussion, call and response vocals in some forms and verse-chorus lyric construction. The most famous Samba figure from Estácio was Ismael Silva. Others were Nilton Bastos, Armando Marçal and Bide. In 1928 the first *Escola de Samba* was formed here. (Escolas de samba are described in detail on the next page.) It was called *Deixa Falar*—let me talk. It would take several chapters to describe the many other legendary composers, lyricists and musicians who made their mark on the development of Samba and Samba styles between the 1920's and the 1950's, but with this brief history you have the beginnings of Samba. There are two other significant topics to keep in mind. The music that had developed to this point—the 1920's—was referred to as *Samba de Morro* by the media and others who found it to be a street, or lower class music. In the 1930's a style called *Samba Cançao* emerged. This style, with its own set of legendary figures, emphasized the lyrics and harmony more than the rhythm. It was developed in middle-class neighborhoods and became the prevalent style from the thirties to the fifties. This style was the predecessor of the Bossa Nova, that sprouted in the fifties, but in the fifties the *Samba de Morro*, which had continued to develop all the while, had a strong resurgence due to the continuing establishment of the *Escola de Samba* as an institution for Carnaval. From its early days, Samba had always been closely tied to *Carnaval*, but it fast became a national institution as well.

Carnaval was initially a Catholic holiday celebrated the week before *Lent*—a period of abstinence lasting four weeks, (biblically speaking, forty days and forty nights). Carnaval was the last chance to go nuts before the Lenten period. Its roots can be traced back to the Bacchanalia of Roman times. Some form of Carnaval is celebrated in most of Latin-America and the Caribbean as well as New Orleans' Mardi Gras in the United States. Carnaval evolved in Brazil from the Portuguese celebration called *Entrudo*. Although present day Carnaval is a time in which anything goes, the Portuguese entrudo of the seventeenth to eighteenth century went much further—to a point that more resembled a street riot. By the nineteenth century the celebration had evolved to incorporate costumery, parading and popular dances of the European aristocracy such as waltzes and polkas. Since much of these celebrations were hosted and enjoyed exclusively by the aristocracy, a movement began in the streets by the poor people that incorporated, among other things, the music that was developing in their same environment. It was the merging of these two cultures that evolved into what became the Brazilian Carnaval.

Since its inception in 1928, the *Escola de Samba* has been an integral part of Carnaval and Brazilian folklore. Literally translated it means school of samba, but these are not schools in the traditional sense. They began as musical clubs or societies where musicians, dancers and the interested general public got together to play music, organize Carnaval parading and partake in other festive activities. Although they presently maintain the same purpose, today their role in Carnaval—and in Brazilian society in general—is more that of a cultural institution. Between 1928 and 1935 the parading through neighborhoods by these early Escolas—the groups of people were referred to as *blocos*—was discouraged and even suppressed by the authorities in keeping with the ongoing suppression of the Afro-Brazilian culture. Nonetheless, the movement persisted and in 1935 the government officially recognized the Escolas and their parades. Consequently the institution of the Escola has not only grown to become a grand spectacle during Carnaval, but Escolas are sometimes the center of community activities in the neighborhoods to which they belong. There are presently some fifty to sixty registered Escolas and countless others that exist purely for the people involved. The official Escolas prepare all year for the competition of the Carnaval parade. The Escolas are judged on their theme— the *Enredo*. This theme can be one of national celebration, protest, or political criticism. Many songs are written about these various themes and each Escola picks one that it will use for that year. The Escolas are also judged on their costumery and their music. An Escola parading in Carnaval can have three to five-thousand members. Additionally there are the many musical arrangers, costume designers, sculptors, painters, organizers and the like, all contributing to this annual two hour parade that the Escola will compete with. The costs for each Escola are sometimes prohibitive since many are comprised of people from poor areas. The financing for much of this comes from various philanthropic individuals and groups from all areas of Brazil's society.

There are very strict guidelines for the Escola's Carnaval presentation. Each section of the Escola is called an *ala*—a wing. There are two mandatory wings—the *Ala de Baianas*—in honor of the *tias* who hosted the *Orixa* worshipping mentioned earlier, and *Comissão de Frente*—the dignitaries or important personalities of the Escola. Everything else is arranged by the *Carnavalesco*—the choreographer of the Escola.

Following is a list of the directors and sections of a typical Escola:

1. **Carnavalesco**—*Artistic Director/Choreographer.*
2. **Ala de Baianas**—*Wing dedicated to the Bahian tias.*
3. **Passistas**—*Master dancers of the Samba for the Escola.*
4. **Porta-Bandeira**—*Flag-bearer of the Escola's flag. A woman.*
5. **Mestre-Sala**—*Master of Ceremonies. A man.*
6. **Carros Alegoricos**—*Decorated parade floats depicting the theme.*
7. **Destaques**—*Members wearing lavish costumes riding atop the floats.*
8. **Diretores de Harmonia**—*Directors, organizers.*
9. **Puxador**—*Lead singer.*

The Porta-Bandeira and the Mestre-Sala are also the most important passistas in the Escola.

Finally there is the **Mestre de Bateria**—the leader of the *Bateria*—the percussion section of the Escola. The typical Bateria can have from three to five-hundred percussionists. Line-ups vary between Escolas but here is a common instrumentation:

> **Surdos:** 30 to 45
> **Caixas:** 40 to 50
> **Repiniques:** 40
> **Pratos:** 10
> **Tamborims:** 70
> **Pandeiros:** 20
> **Ago-gos:** 20 to 30
> **Cuicas:** 20 to 25
> **Chocalos:** 50
> **Reco-recos:** 25

The Mestre de Bateria leads the percussion section with a whistle and the repinique. (See the next chapter for an instrument list and descriptions.)

The parade begins with the Escola singing the enredo unaccompanied two or three times. This is led by the *puxador* who will keep these five-thousand voices in sync for close to two hours without making a mistake. Then the entrance of the Bateria occurs. This is a truly powerful moment. The Comissaó de Frente steps into the Sambódromo—the Sambadrome—and the various alas and floats begin to parade in. The Bateria enters following, roughly, the first half of the Escola. The judges are seated along the middle of the way. The Bateria stops and plays before the judges while the second half of the Escola parades by. When the last ala has passed they close the parade. By this time the next Escola is beginning enter. During the course of the parade the Bateria performs many breaks for the voices to sing unaccompanied, as well as performing many soloistic breaks on the percussion instruments. To play with three-hundred other percussionists in a group of five-thousand is truly the ultimate in ensemble performance. It is one of the most impressive and beautiful things you can ever hope to see or hear.

Baiaó and other Northern Styles

While the Baiáo is probably the most well-known style from the north of Brazil, the term *northern style* generally refers to styles from regions well north of the state of Bahia. If you're simply speaking of regions north of Rio, you are including a vast territory and the music from these regions is in fact music from the north. But when referring to the northern styles in a more traditional Brazilian way, it is actually the music from north of Bahia that is being referred to. When a Brazilian musician tells me that this is a style from the north they are generally referring to music such as Candomble, Afoxé, Xaxado or Coco—styles that developed in the regions of Recife in the state of Pernambuco. For our purposes we'll take the more general approach and briefly describe some key areas that have produced rhythm styles and artists worth noting.

Moving directly north from Rio you enter the state of Minas Gerais, a land known for its wealth of mineral resources. While not having styles as well known as Samba or Bossa Nova, many innovative composers and instrumentalists fare from this region. Milton Nascimento (born in Rio but raised in Minas Gerais), Toninho Horta, and Wagner Tiso are three of the most well known. The social customs of Minas are generally more subdued than in Rio and the region is said to have a quiet and mystical quality about it when compared to Rio, Bahia or Saó Paolo. It is easy to hear this influence in the music of Milton and Toninho, but musicians from this region are also well known for incorporating the influences of many styles into their music to develop into their own very unique Brazilian styles. Along with other popular Brazilian musicians they began developing these styles in Belo Horizonte, the capital of Minas.

Moving north from Minas you enter the state of Bahia. In 1549, Portugal's colonial government for Brazil was established in the northern port city that would become Salvador, the capital of Bahia. (Salvador went on to become the capital of Brazil until 1763.) Over the next three centuries, thousands of Africans were brought to this area to work the cocoa and sugar plantations established by the Portuguese. Most of the Africans brought were Yoruban. This is the predominant Afro-Brazilian culture in this region and this region has the highest concentration of African descendants in Brazil. This region maintains the most African heritage of any area of Brazil. Salvador, its capital, is said to be the most African of all Brazilian cities. Candomble, Capoeira and Afoxé are all very alive in this region and have been integrated with many other styles of music from Brazil, the Caribbean and the United States to form newer Afro-Brazilian styles. Carnaval parades and festivities in these regions are thoroughly Africanized, mostly featuring these song forms. Although most known for these musical styles, many famous Samba and Bossa Nova artists originally came from this region. One of the most popular songwriters from this region is Dorival Caymmi who based many of his pieces on the folklore and regional styles of Bahia. In addition to these folkloric styles, this region gave birth—actually a rebirth—to the Baião and its many derivations. The traditional, folkloric Baião was the music that accompanied an African circle dance, but in the mid-forties, an accordionist named Luiz Gonzaga, (originally from the state of Pernambuco), recorded a song called Baião that he had co-composed with Humberto Teixeira. A new dance and musical style emerged and became extremely popular almost immediately. Gonzaga is known as the king of Baião. He also popularized other regional styles like the *Xaxado*, *Xote* and *Coco*. Another historic musical figure from these parts is Jackson do Pandeiro, known for his development of the *Coco* and the *Embolada*.

Moving even further north is the area of Recife in the state of Pernambuco. This region is also steeped in the African tradition and song forms. Another style called *Frevo* was developed here and later in Bahia. This style features extremely fast tempos and much instrumental improvisation. Also from this region is the *Maracatu*, an Afro-Brazilian processional dance derived from the *Congadas* also popular during Carnaval in Recife. There is also Indian tradition that survives in this region. The *Caboclinho* groups are dedicated to the depiction of Brazil's native Indians during the periods of Portuguese colonization. They also participate in the Carnaval parades of these regions wearing Indian costumes and performing music that is derived from the Indian heritage of these regions.

The musical styles from the northern regions of Brazil have not enjoyed the world-wide recognition that the Samba and Bossa have, but they have had the strongest influence on the development of all Brazilian styles and have also influenced the music of Caribbean and South American styles in this general area. There is a bottomless pit of rhythms and songstyles to explore from this area.

Now onward with the musical examples.

The Percussion Instruments

The following is a list of the more common percussion instruments from Brazil:

Surdo (3 Types) _____*Bass Drum used for Samba.*

1. Surdo Marcaçào _*Lowest, largest surdo. Also called the Surdo Marcaná. Measures approximately 20" x 22" or 22" x 24".*

2. Surdo Resposta __*Middle-pitched, middle-sized Surdo. Also called the Contra-Surdo. Measures approximately 15" x 16" or 16" x 18".*

3. Surdo Cortador __*Highest pitched and smallest sized Surdo. Measures approximately 12" x 13" or 13" x 14".*

Zabumba_____*Bass Drum used for Baiaó and other northern styles.*

Ago-go _____*Ago-go Bells.*

Triangulo _____*Triangle.*

Caixeta _____*Wood Block or Temple Block.*

Chocalo _____*Metal canister shakers.*

Ganza_____*Weaved basket shakers.*

Cabasa_____*Gourd shaped with a handle and beads wrapped around it.*

Reco-reco _____*Metal scratcher.*

Tamborim_____*Small tambourine-shaped instrument without jingles played with a multi-pronged stick.*

Pandeiro _____*Brazilian tambourine.*

Apito_____*Samba whistle.*

Cuica _____*Friction drum. Also called a lion's roar.*

Repinique/Repique ____*Small high pitched double headed drum used to play solo cue the Escola de Samba.*

Atabaque (3 Types) ____*Conga type hand drums used in Candomble and similar Afro-Brazilian styles.*

1. Rum _____*Largest of the Atabaque.*

2. Rumpi_____*Middle-sized drum.*

3. Lê _____*Smallest of the Atabaque.*

Caxixi_____*Small weaved basket shakers originally used with the Berimbau in Capoeira music.*

Berimbau _____*Bow-shaped instrument originally used to accompany Capoeira dancing. Played with a small stick, caxixi and a coin or metal washer.*

Caixa _____*Snare Drum.*

Pratos_____*Cymbals.*

Tips for Getting the Right Sound and Feel on the Percussion Instruments

You may have to acquaint yourself with some concepts that may be unfamiliar to you in order to get the right sound. Some are of a technical nature, others are more interpretive.

When you strike a drum, or any part of a drum set or percussion instrument, you have at least three considerations that will affect the type of sound you'll get. One is what part of the stick you are playing with—the tip, the shoulder or the butt end. The second is what type of stroke you use—an upstroke, downstroke, open stroke, dead-sticking stroke, accented, unaccented, loud, soft, ghosted. Third is what part of the surface you strike. Virtually any part of the instrument can be played—not just the usual parts. Try experimenting with this. You may hear yourself playing sounds you've never played before. Getting the right sound and feel in these styles requires the use of these various stroke types—particularly dead-sticking, use of the shoulder of the stick on the ride cymbal or hi-hat, and rim shots and buzz strokes.

The same myriad of sounds are available on instruments that you play with your bare hand. The shape of your hand, what part of the hand strikes the surface and what part of the surface you play all create different sounds. It is necessary to develop control of all the various sounds in order to make the patterns you play feel right and to have a broad variety of sounds at your disposal.

In terms of musical concepts, the way you feel and play each particular style will be different, but there are some general things common to many Brazilian styles—or at least to styles of a given region. Styles from the northeast share certain characteristics, as do various Samba styles. There will be more specific detail on each style in its respective chapter but here are some general feel factors to keep in mind.

Phrase to the last note of the bar, and the beat, whether in a time feel, fill, or in parts of solo phrases. This gives a feeling of forward motion to the groove, rather than playing the downbeats, which give a feeling of cadence to the time. Here are two examples:

1.
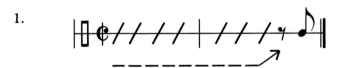

2.
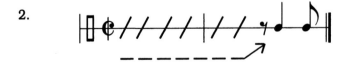

This illustrates the previous concepts in two very common rhythmic phrases used in many Brazilian styles:

1.

2.

If you learn to stick the following phrase correctly, you will be very close to capturing the essence of the Samba rhythm. The key is to slur the three right hand strokes and pull back a little on the time.

Another common element in all Sambas is the short, unaccented note on the downbeat and the longer, heavier note on the upbeat of each bar.

Here are two rhythmic inflections common to many styles from the northeastern regions.

1.   2.

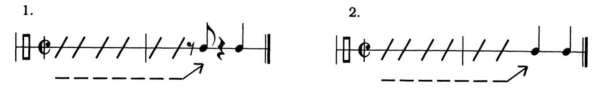

All of these rhythmic elements are very general, but they are integral components in getting the right sound and feel. Listen for them in the music you hear in this idiom. Practice playing time feels and improvising around each of these.

Surdo

The surdo is a wood or metal barrel-shaped drum with heads on both sides. The heads can be calf-skin or plastic. It is played with a mallet in one hand and the fingers and palm of the other hand. The mallet is made of either felt or natural animal hide and possibly some filler material covering a wooden beater. While one hand strikes the drum with the mallet, the other mutes and/or plays some supportive or decorative rhythms around the main pulse. Surdos are most commonly and traditionally used in Escolas de Samba where three types—and many of each type— are used. An Escola typically has twenty-five to thirty-five surdos in its Bateria. Pictured above are various sizes and mallets.

There are many actual sizes of surdos, but they all fall under three basic categories:

1. **Surdo Marcaná** *or* **Surdo Marcaçáo.** This is the largest and lowest pitched of the three surdos. It is responsible for playing the stronger (and lower pitched) upbeat of the Samba. It is the predominant surdo responsible for carrying the bass or foundation rhythm. These drums measure approximately 20" x 22" or 22" x 24'.

2. **Surdo Resposta** *or* **Contra-surdo.** This is the middle size and middle pitched drum of the three. It plays the lighter downbeats of the Samba rhythm. This drum would only be used if the large drum—the marcaná—is used. These drums measure approximately 15" x 16" or 16" x 18".

3. **Surdo-Cortador.** This is the smallest size and highest pitched drum. Cortador
   means cutting. This is what this drum's part does. The syncopations and variations
   of the Samba are played on this drum. It cuts between the more stable ostinato rhythms of
   the other two drums. It is also mostly used in large ensembles.
   These drums measure approximately 12" x 13" or 13" x 14".

All three Surdos are usually used in large ensembles. In small groups, all of the rhythms are usually played on one large surdo by one player. The patterns played and what the left hand does depends on whether all three surdos are playing, or just one player is playing alone. Although when only one person is playing, all the parts are usually played on one large surdo, more than one drum can be used. This gives one player a more traditional orchestration as well as more melodic possibilities.

Again, the surdo plays the bass rhythm. It provides the foundation for the entire Escola—and the entire Samba. There are four basic strokes used to play the surdo:

1. *The left hand strikes the surdo. This stroke can mute the head or play
   an open tone—(figure 1).*

2. *The right hand strikes the surdo with the mallet with no muting from the left hand.
   This would be an open tone —(figure 2).*

3. *The right hand strikes the surdo with the left hand muting the head.
   This would be a closed tone—(figure 3).*

4. *The right hand strikes the rim of the drum with the shaft of the stick.
   Depending on where you are in the pattern, your left hand may or may not
   be muting the head during this stroke—(figure 4).*

Figure 1

Figure 2

Figure 3

Figure 4

The following sections show surdo rhythms for specific songstyles.

Samba Patterns for Surdo

The samba is always felt and played in two no matter what the tempo is. The foundation rhythm for the samba is basically the downbeats of the bar. In cut time, the one and the two. The foundation rhythm looks like this:

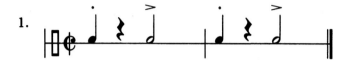

The first note, the one, is short and dead—muted. The second note, the two (see *figure 2* on previous page for hand position), is long and accented. The feeling is as if the downbeat were on the upbeat of the bar. This is not only the way the surdo rhythm is played, but the way the samba feels. You should learn to feel the style this way with your entire body so that you will project an authentic and strong feel. Following is the most common variation of the basic pattern.

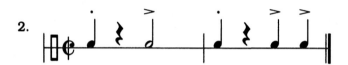

A large Escola de Samba may have many surdos playing simultaneously. When this happens, the medium-size *Contra Surdos* (surdos resposta), play the downbeats—the ones, the small, high *Surdo Cortador* plays the syncopations and variations, and the low, *Surdos Marcaná* plays the up-beats—the twos. Remember that beat two is the strong, accented beat. Following is an example of the way two and three surdo sizes would play in ensemble.

The patterns of the surdo cortador in the following example would vary based on the specific songstyle and tempo and/or the improvisations of the player..

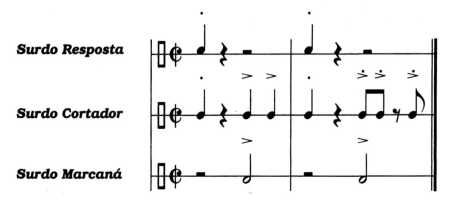

When only one surdo is playing, or when only one size is used in ensemble, that player or players play the entire pattern. Following are some basic surdo patterns for the samba. The top line is for the hand holding the mallet—usually the right hand. The bottom line shows the left hand function. Note that when the left hand *note-head "x"* falls with a note in the top line, it is muting the head while the mallet strikes the drum. When the left hand falls opposite the right—playing by itself—it is most often playing *filler* or *ghosted* notes between the main notes of the samba pattern played by the right hand. When the left hand note is in parenthesis it indicates both the starting position of the pattern and the muting of the head as the pattern continues. Also note the *long* and *short* articulation markings for the top line.

1.

2.

3.

4.

5.

6.

There are many variations and much improvising that can be done around the basic framework, but the fundamental underlying rhythmic pattern must be maintained, as it is the foundation for the entire Samba. When practicing these patterns keep in mind that it is impossible to notate every nuance that takes place in actual performance. Experiment and listen to the recorded examples as well as commercial recordings. If the Samba is slow, the left hand is used for additional dampening of short notes. This also creates other rhythmic articulations. If the pattern is fast, the notes in parenthesis, (ex. 3 & 4 on the previous page), are played by the left hand slightly before the downbeat. This becomes more like a two-handed pattern.

Following are common licks for beginnings, endings, breaks and variations of the groove. It is very common to start the Samba on the *and* or with the *2-and* as shown in the first two examples.

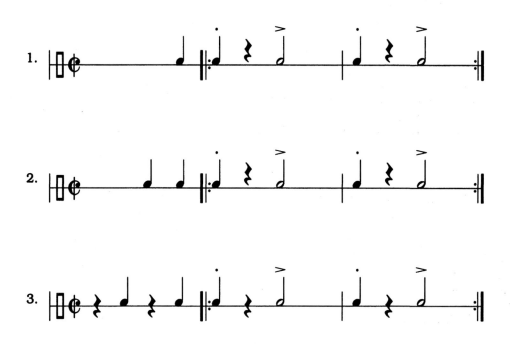

In the following example, the first note feels like it is the downbeat when you first hear it, when in fact it is the upbeat. This is also a very common variation.

The following example is a rhythmic cliché for beginning and ending a Batucada.

It is also very common to use the rim of the drum for part of the rhythm pattern. You will have two sounds on the rim. One we'll call a *closed rim sound* and one an *open rim sound*. Closed and open are determined by the muting done with the left hand. The most common pattern has the rim playing on the *ands*.

Here is a Rhythmic Key for the following patterns:

RH–Rim Stroke–closed
RH–Head Stroke-closed
RH–Head Stroke-open
LH–Head Stroke-closed
LH–Muting for RH Stroke

1.

2.

Baiaó Patterns for the Surdo or Zabumba

The bass pattern of the Baiaó is played on the surdo or a drum called the Zabumba. Like the surdo, the Zabumba is also played with a mallet and the bare hand. This drum is not as common as the surdo traditionally used for samba, although it is quite common in some styles from the north of Bahia.

Following are two very common patterns used for Baiaó. The rhythms on the top line are played with the mallet. Those on the bottom indicate the notes you mute with the hand.

1.

2.
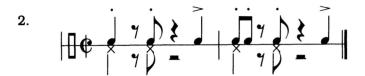

Following are three very common one bar variations. They are integrated into longer phrases in the next set of examples.

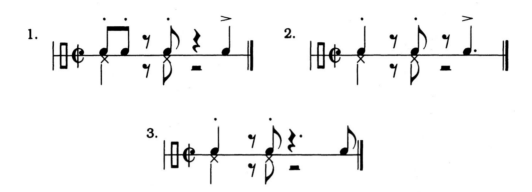

These are patterns commonly used as variations to the basic time feel or as the third and/or fourth bars of a four bar phrase. All have a basic pattern in the first two bars with variations in the third and/or fourth bars.

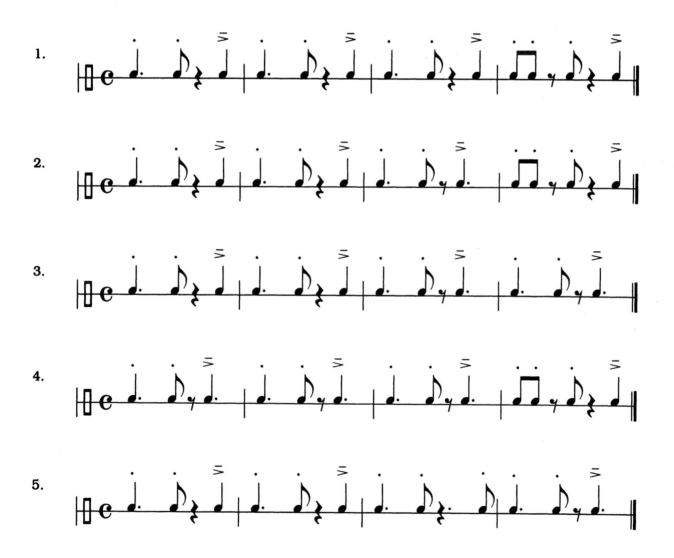

Ago-go Bells

Ago-go bells are pairs of bells connected with a metal rod. There are also sets of three or four bells connected together. They are usually tuned in thirds, held in one hand, and played with a stick with the other. Once a rhythm is started, the pattern is generally kept constant except in less traditional settings where improvising variations works well.

Following are some common patterns for Samba:

1.

2.

3.

The first of these next two patterns is common for Baiaó. The second—its reverse—is also used as both a pattern and a variation:

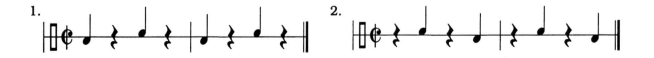

The following pattern is played for the Maracatu:

This pattern is common for the Marcha de Rancho:

Another very common technique is that of squeezing the bells together with the connecting rod to produce a *chick* sound *(figure 1)*. The sound can be used as rhythmic filler played in between the sticked notes *(figure 2)*. You can also hold the bells together while you hit them, giving you muted notes *(figure 3)*. These notes become part of the pattern itself. Following are some examples. *The notes marked "X" are played by squeezing the bells together for the "chick" sound. The others are played with the stick on the high and low bells.*

Figure 1

Figure 2

Figure 3

1.　　　　　　　　　　　　　　　　　　2.

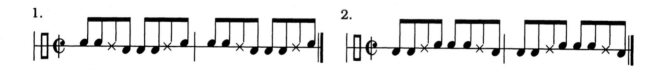

3.

As with all the percussion instruments in all the various songstyles, the possibilities for rhythms are endless. Listed here are only a few common patterns. Improvise to come up with your own patterns and licks. To get going you can try starting patterns 1-3 above on the second bar.

Triangle

The triangle was originally more common in the Baiaó, but now it is also common for samba and other styles. It is played with a metal beater. There are several ways of holding and playing it:

1. *Held using a triangle clip—striking inner side to side (figure 1).*
2. *Hand-held directly—striking inner side to side (figure 2).*
3. *Hand-held directly—striking corner to corner (figure 3).*
4. *Hand-held directly—striking outer side (figure 4).*

Figure 1

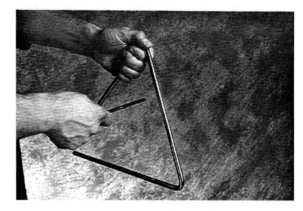

Figure 2

Figure 3

Figure 4

The rhythmic pattern is a combination of the striking of the triangle and the muting done with the left hand. This creates the open and closed tones. Following are some examples to practice. Number one is the most commonly used groove. Numbers two and three have differences that work better in subtle situations or in a studio with close miking. They are also good as technical exercises.

Notes marked with a "+" are muted. The "o" means an open, non-muted stroke.

1.
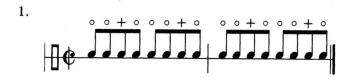

2.
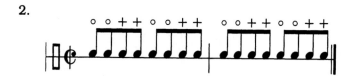

3.

The following are variations for playing grooves striking the outer side of the triangle:

1.
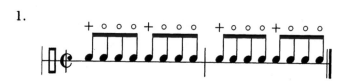

2.

Caixeta

 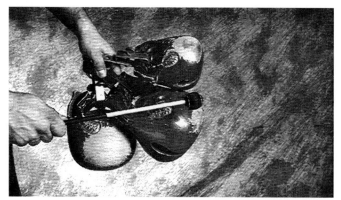

A Caixeta is a wood block or temple block. It is played with a stick or mallet. There is nothing complicated about playing this other than making the rhythms groove right and getting a good tone. One derivative of this sound is the rim-click sound used in drum set playing. The following patterns can be used for Samba or Baiaó at any tempo.

For more variations you can start all of the above patterns on the second bar. If more than one wood block or temple block is used you can break up the patterns between the two pitches.

Chocalo and Ganza

Figure 1   *Figure 2*   *Figure 3*

A chocalo is a canister shaker. A ganza is a shaker made from weaved baskets. (Caxixi could also fall under this category, but we'll deal with them in a section of their own.) Since the baskets are mostly handmade, they come in many different shapes and sizes as do the metal shakers. They are usually filled with sand or lead pebbles. The canister is most commonly metal, but can be made of plastic. Sometimes two or three metal canisters are welded together for the big sound needed by an Escola de Samba performing in Carnaval (*figure 1 shows various types*). They are held with one hand, in the center (*figure 2*), or with both hands at the ends (*figure 3*). It seems obvious that you play it by shaking, but there is a certain feel you must get out of the eighth notes. You must also be able to accent as well as ghost some of the notes. There are also many tricks you can develop to get interesting licks with one or two shakers simultaneously. First try to play even eighth notes, then add the accents. Try playing the downbeats away from you and the *ands* towards you. At slower tempos use bigger motions. At brighter tempos, wrist strokes are more effective. Accents are little snaps of the wrist.

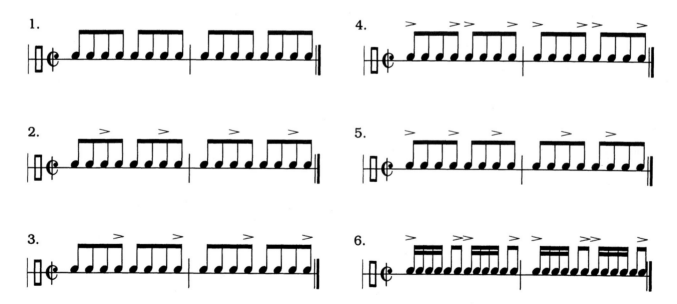

For this last example you need a long and large shaker whose beads move slowly from one end to the other as you tilt the ends. The second bar is played by lowering one end and letting the beads roll to the other end for the duration of a whole note.

Afoxé, Xequeré, and Cabasa

Figure 1: Various traditional versions

Figure 2: Newer variations

Traditional Afoxés and Xequeré (Shekeré) are made from gourds, so there are many different shapes and sizes due to it being a natural material. Certain musical styles require specific sizes and types of these instruments. The shape of the gourd for the Brazilian Afoxé varies, but the more common shape consists of a round part of a gourd which forms the head, and a part that tapers down into a handle. The head has plastic beads weaved or wrapped around it usually tied with string or cord (*figure 1*). Shekerés tend to be larger in size, producing a bigger sound—especially in the bass tone produced by hitting the closed end with the heel of the hand. Most cabasas made today have wooden handles with wood and metal heads and metal beads on the head (*figure 2*). These newer ones produce a much different sound than those made of gourd. Though very different, they do have a sound that has been incorporated into a lot of Brazilian as well as other styles of music.

There are also almost as many ways to play cabasas as there are varieties of them. In the most basic approach, the right hand holds the handle and turns the cabasa. The left hand holds the head—the beads. The friction of the beads against the gourd produces the sound and the sliding of the beads as the cabasa is turned produces the accents and rhythm (*figure 3*). Another method involves shaking the cabasa and playing tones with the palm of the hand on the closed part of the head (*figure 4*).

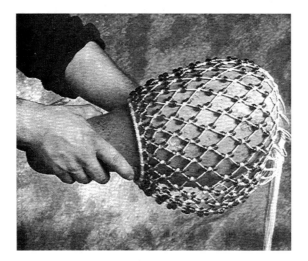

Figure 3

Figure 4

With the head of the cabasa sitting in the palm of your hand, turn the cabasa and practice articulating even eighth notes first. Then practice the following patterns. A sharper turn and additional pressure will produce accents.

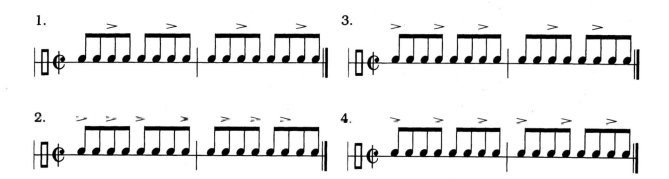

Another very different sound is produced by holding the head upright and shaking the cabasa back and forth (*figure 5a*). This produces sharper and shorter notes. With this method, (holding the cabasa in the right hand), the left hand is used to play rhythms and/or syncopate. Use the palm and heel of the left hand. I play the cabasa into the palm of my left hand for forward—downbeat—accents (*figure 5b*), and bring the left hand around and strike the cabasa with the heel of my hand as it is moving back towards me for the upbeat accents (*figure 5c*). A long tone is produced by striking the top of the head—the beads—and simultaneously turning the right hand in towards you while moving the arm up and away from you and then back down, allowing the beads to rotate freely (*figure 5d*). This takes some doing to get it happening consistently.

Figure 5a

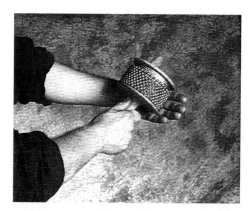

Figure 5b

Figure 5c

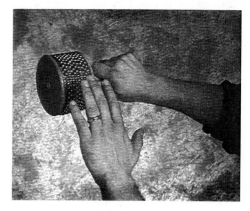

Figure 5d

Practice the following patterns. First try to articulate even eighths, then add the accents. Try the downbeat accents playing forward and into your hand, and the upbeat accents back towards you and with the heel of your hand. Improvise your own patterns. The possibilities are endless. The line on the tied note in example four is a long note played by spinning the beads.

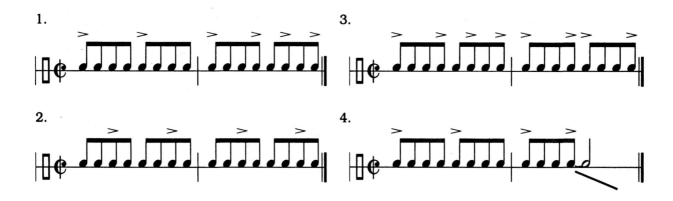

Here is a four bar example combining the examples above:

Experiment with the above combinations and make up your own patterns. You don't have to limit yourself to *cut time*. Here is an example in seven followed by one in five. Various odd-time approaches are discussed later in the book.

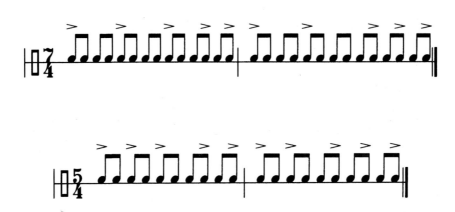

Reco-Reco

Figure 1

Figure 2

The reco-reco is basically a scratcher. Most are made of either a metal box with ridges cut into the top side or a metal tube with springs extended across its length (*figure 1*). They are most commonly used in Escolas de Samba. It mostly resembles the effect that scratching a washboard would have. It is played by sliding a metal, wood or rattan stick against the ridges (*figure 2*). The stick almost never leaves the ridges. Patterns consist mostly of continuous eighth notes with additional pressure for the accents. Where quarter notes appear, the scratches should be longer. Practice the following patterns, first trying to play consistent eighth notes, then adding the accents.

Basic Samba

Maracatu

Baião

Marcha

Here are some variations:

1.

4.

2.

5.

3.

6.

Tamborim

Figure 1

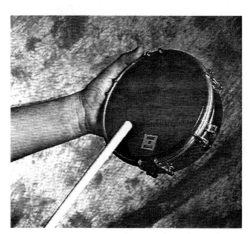

Figure 2

The tamborim is similar in shape to a miniature tambourine but with no jingles. It is played with a thin wooden stick or a three-pronged plastic or rattan stick. The fingers of the hand holding the tamborim are also used to dampen the back side of the head to produce open or closed notes (*figure 1*). There are two ways it is commonly played. The first and most basic is to play the top of the head with the stick (*figure 2*), adjusting the open and close the notes with the fingers on the underside of the head. Different stroke types are also used for a variety of sounds: 1. *Tip of stick in center of head*, 2. *Rim shots*, 3. *Rim shots with shoulder of stick*, 4. *Accents*. In Escolas performing in Carnaval several are used in unison to orchestrate rhythmic passages.

Practice the following patterns. The notes marked with a "+" are played with the fingers muting the head. Those marked with an "o" are open notes with no muting.

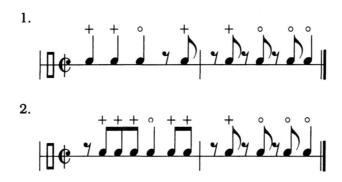

3.

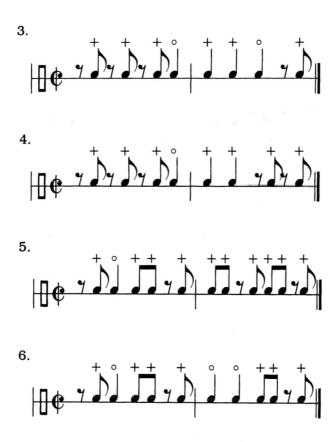

4.

5.

6.

As an additional embellishment, the fingers may also play a *filler* rhythm on the underside of the head. These notes play between the notes being struck by the stick. This creates more of a two-handed pattern. The finger notes function like *ghosted* notes. Following are two examples:

1.

2.

The second way to play the tamborim involves a little more technique. Traditionally this approach is played with a three-pronged beater (*shown in examples below*), although it can also be done with a regular stick depending on the sound desired. The other hand rotates the tamborim so the beater strikes in two different spots (*figures 3a through 3c*). This gives you accented and unaccented notes to produce the samba pattern notated below. Following is the most common rhythm played with this technique.

This pattern would be played on two parts of the tamborim. The notes marked "R" in the pattern would be played at the bottom of the tamborim as shown in (*figure 3a*). This is similar to the first technique presented on the previous page. The stroke marked "L" in the pattern is played at the top of the tamborim and is executed by the other hand *rotating* the tamborim to meet the stick. You can think of this stroke as being played by the left hand striking the stick (when it rotates the tamborim), instead of the stick striking the tamborim (*figures 3b and 3c*).

Figure 3a   Figure 3b   Figure 3c

Pandeiro

The Pandeiro is the Brazilian tambourine. This is an instrument that requires considerable technique to play. It has been developed and mastered by various musicians to the point of true artistry. The pandeiro is very often a featured solo instrument in Escolas de Samba, as well as in contemporary groups where a percussionist is featured. Traditional Carnaval solos often include theatrical tricks such as rolling the tambourine across the chest, or down the leg and off the foot, spinning them on the tip of the fingers or playing two tambourines simultaneously. A musician by the name of Joaó de Baiana (Joaó Machado Guedes) is said to have introduced the pandeiro as an instrument in the Escola de Samba.

Pandeiros can have plastic or calf-skin heads. They come in different sizes with 10" and 12" being the most common. Calf-skin heads produce a better sound, but present tuning problems as the weather changes so plastic heads are more common.

The pandeiro is held in the weak hand. The fingers, thumb and heel of the other hand are used to strike the top of the head. Open and closed tones are governed by either the thumb or middle finger of the hand holding the tambourine. The thumb can mute and release from the top of the head (*figure 1*). The middle finger can mute and release from the underside of the head (*figure 2*). Which method you use depends on the type of groove you're playing, the size of the pandeiro, and what you're most comfortable with.

Figure 1

Figure 2

Following is a notation code for the rhythmic patterns:

1. *Thumb stroke near edge of head. Similar to a rim shot. This will be either an open or closed tone (figure 1).*

2. *Finger stroke in the upper center of the head. Use the tips of the first three fingers (figure 2).*

2a. *There is another technique used with this stroke. The left hand pivots or rotates the tambourine side to side. This can be thought of as the tambourine striking the fingers instead of the fingers striking the tambourine. In actual playing it is a combination of the two motions (figure 2a).*

3. *Thumb stroke or heel of hand in lower center of head (figure 3).*

4. *Finger stroke—same as number two (figure 4). *A number 4 stroke notated with an accent means the note is a slap stroke.*

Figure 1

Figure 2

Figure 2a

Figure 3

Figure 4

Practice the following exercises. In these initial exercises the left hand only holds the pandeiro (assuming you are right-handed, otherwise reverse). The bottom note only indicates the rhythmic inflection you should make with the right hand. Focus on playing with the correct hand positions in your right hand. Accented, unaccented, and ghosted notes play an essential part in the groove. For the basic Samba groove, your most prominent accent will be a slight accent or slap on the fourth subdivision of each beat.

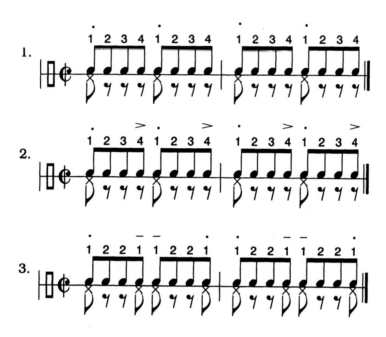

Following are two basic Samba patterns. The main difference between the two is the accent in the second one.

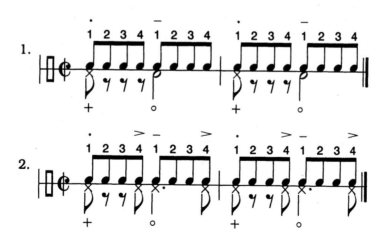

Here are six variations for the Samba rhythm. The bottom line is showing you the rhythmic outline of the notes emphasized by the right hand. It also shows you when and when not to mute the head to play the open and closed tones indicated.

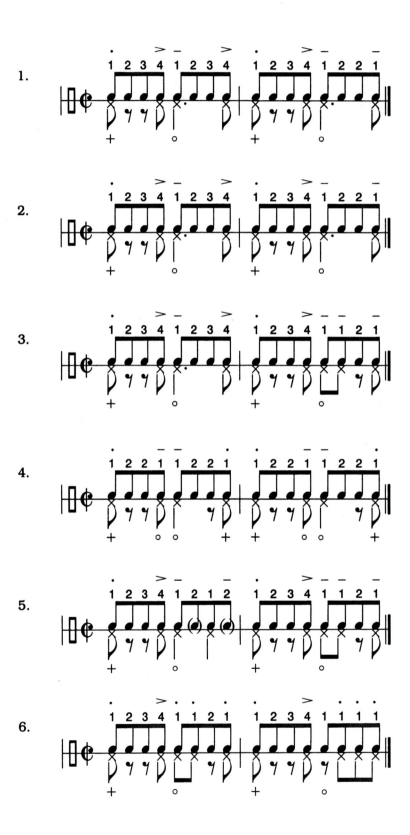

The following pattern is for a rhythm called Maxixe:

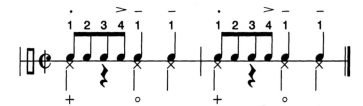

The following patterns are for a Marcha:

1.

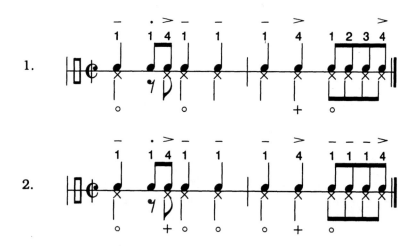

2.

This pattern can be used for playing Frevo:

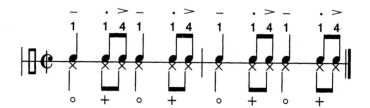

The following two patterns can be used for the Samba de Partido Alto:

1.

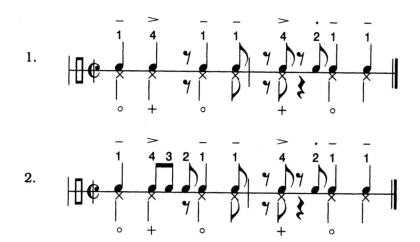

2.

Following are some basic odd time rhythmic patterns for pandeiro. These meters are not as common as cut time, but are common in contemporary compositions. The basic samba framework is still in the pattern even though the left hand is not notated. Use the articulation markings as your guide for playing the open and closed tones.

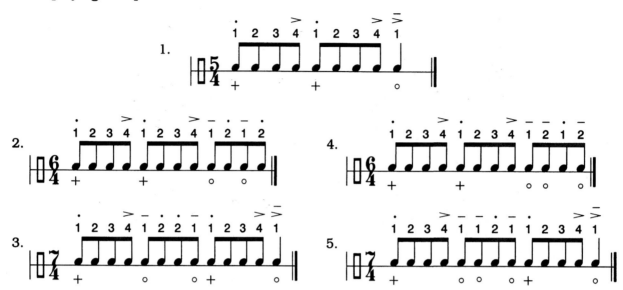

Following is another technique for playing the pandeiro. This is actually the most basic, and easiest way to play a Samba groove. In this method, you move the tambourine up and down with the left hand between the strokes of the right hand (*figures 1 & 2*). The notes between the finger strokes are sounded by the jingles as you shake the pandeiro up and down.

Figure 1

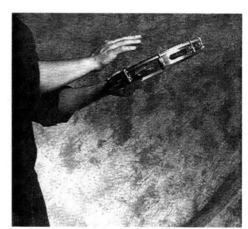

Figure 2

Following is a common pattern for Samba.

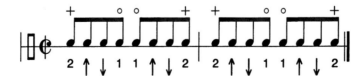

Here is one for the Baião:

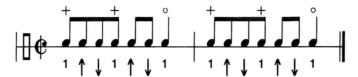

Apito

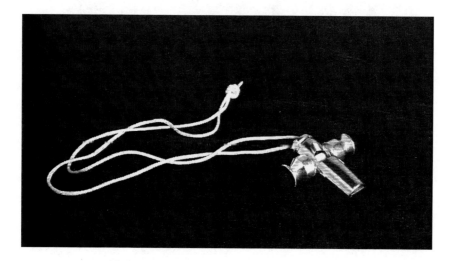

Apito is the word for whistle—in this case, the Brazilian Samba whistle. It was traditionally carved from wood. Today's whistles are made of metals like brass. The whistle has holes on its sides which are covered and uncovered with the fingers to produce different tones as you blow into it. The apito is used both to play rhythmic patterns and to announce either an ensemble passage, a new section, a beginning, or the end of a piece. In an Escola de Samba, the *Mestre de Bateria* would give these cues. To him the whistle, along with the repinique (presented later in the book), is like the conductor's baton. The apito is capable of producing loud and soft, long and short, and open and closed tones. All of them are used to add variety and color to the patterns played. The whistle can also play a repetitive pattern that functions as part of the entire ensemble's rhythm.

Cuica

The cuica is an instrument whose origins are less known than that of the other Afro-Brazilian instruments. It was brought to Brazil by African—probably Bantú—slaves but can be traced to other northern regions of Africa as well as the Iberian peninsula. It is also called the *lion's roar, friction drum* and less commonly, the *puíta*. In its early incarnations it was also used by hunters luring lions with the growls the instrument can produce. There are many sizes of cuicas, and although generally categorized as a percussion instrument, the cuica is not struck. It is a metal or wood canister with a calf-skin head on the top side. Embedded on the underside of the head is a bamboo post. The thumb, index, and middle fingers of one hand hold the rod on the cuica's interior with a small piece of damp cloth. The rhythm is articulated by the pushing and pulling along the length of the rod (*figure 1*). The other hand helps hold the cuica and with the fingers or thumb exerts pressure on the head (*figure 2 and 3*). The pressure is exerted close to the rod on the top side of the head. The tighter you hold the rod, and the more pressure you exert on the head, the higher the pitch. A looser grip and less pressure on the head produces lower tones. The pitch range of the cuica can be as much as two octaves. In Brazilian music the tones produced tend to imitate the voice in the form of grunts, groans, moans, and squeaking sounds. It can also provide a rhythmic ostinato. After becoming integrated in the Brazilian percussion arsenal, the cuica was traditionally used by the Escolas de Samba for Carnaval, but is currently also used in contemporary jazz, Latin and funk styles. When marching in an Escola a strap is used to hang the cuica from the neck or shoulder.

Figure 1

Figure 2

Figure 3

Practice the following rhythms. Try to get two pitches and keep them constant. Gradually try to extend the range and use more pitches in the patterns.

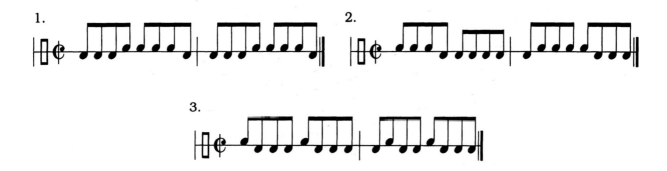

Here are some more syncopated patterns:

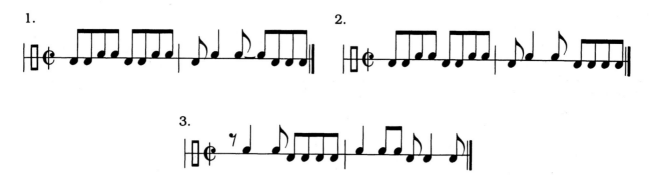

Here are some common licks:

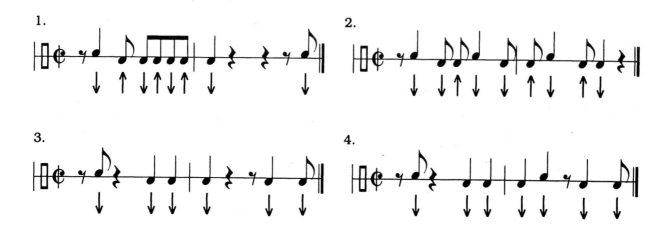

Atabaque, Congas and other Hand Drums

Figure 1: Atabaque. L—R: Lé, Rumpi and Rum

Figure 2: Contemporary Congas and Bongos

Atabaque are Afro-Brazilian hand drums—conga like drums—that are indigenous to the northern style of Candomble and related traditions. These songstyles remain most linked and influenced by the African Yoruba tradition. There are three Atabaque, the *Lé, Rumpi* and the *Rum (figure 1)*. Their traditional use was in ritual and religious music; they were used to summon the *Orixas*—the gods of the Candomble religion. Some contemporary styles from the north also now include them in their music. They are played with the hands, two sticks or sometimes with one stick and the hand depending on the rhythm and the drum you are playing. More generic contemporary hand drums *(figure 2)*—congas and bongos—are common for Samba, Baiaó, and other contemporary styles such as Brazilian jazz, funk and their off-shoots. It is now very common to hear adaptations of common Brazilian rhythms played on congas and bongos. Keep in mind that if you want to play hand drums you need to develop the techniques of these instruments. You have to have at least the following basic stroke types down to play the hand drums: ***bass tone, open tones, closed and palm tones, slap (3 types: open, closed, and muted),*** and the ***rocking motion between the heel and fingers of the hand.*** Examples of these techniques are illustrated on the next page.

Following is a set of rhythms for the Atabaque based on the Afoxé style.

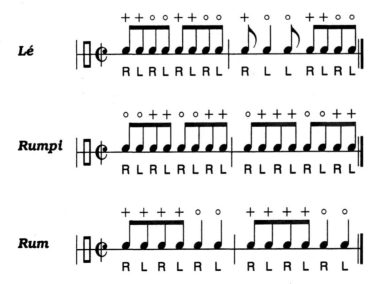

Following are examples of the basic hand stroke types for the conga drums.

Figure 1

Figure 2

Figure 3

Bass Tones: Played with the heel of the hand on the center of the drum *(figures 1 and 2)*. If you're playing sitting down and holding the drum with your legs, you can pick it up off the floor to get more sound *(figures 3 and 4)*.

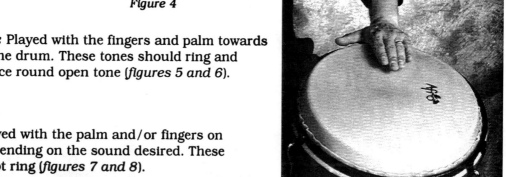

Figure 4

Open Tones: Played with the fingers and palm towards the edge of the drum. These tones should ring and produce a nice round open tone *(figures 5 and 6)*.

Closed and Palm Tones: Played with the palm and/or fingers on various places of the head depending on the sound desired. These tones should be muted and not ring *(figures 7 and 8)*.

Figure 5

Figure 6

Figure 7

Figure 8

Figure 9

Figure 10

Figure 11

Heel-Toe Rocking Motion: Played by rocking between the heel and toe (fingertips) of the hand. These tones do not ring. They are the double strokes of the hand drums. (*Figures 9 and 10 are the Left Hand sequence. Figures 11 and 12 are the Right Hand sequence.*)

Slap Tones 3 types: **Closed,** played by slapping the head and holding it so the tone is closed (*figures 13 and 14*). **Open,** played by slapping the head and releasing the hand from the head allowing the tone to ring (*figures 15 and 16*). **Muted,** played by slapping the head and muting it with the other hand (*figures 17 and 18*).

Figure 12

Closed Slaps

Open Slaps

Muted Slaps

Figure 13

Figure 15

Figure 17

Figure 14

Figure 16

Figure 18

The following patterns will sound good with most of the songstyles presented in this book. They will also work in a more generic Latin-jazz situation where you want to play a conga or bongo rhythm with a Brazilian flavor.

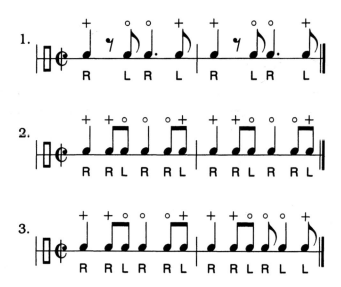

This pattern comes from the Partido Alto. The notation code is as follows:

O = Open Tone
P = Palm (closed) Tone
S = Slap
H = Heel Stroke of Rocking Motion
T = Toe stroke of Rocking Motion

These two are for the Baião:

This pattern is for the Bongos. Basically the same notation code as above applies except that on the bongos the heel/toe rocking motion is played more with the thumb and fingers and the right (R) strokes can be played with either one, two, three fingers or the whole hand depending on the sound texture you want.

Caixa

The caixa's (snare drum's) use in Afro-Brazilian styles has its roots in the Portuguese military parade styles. The caixa's most prevalent role is in the Samba Marcha, the Batucada and related Carnaval styles, although it is also included in many other songstyles. By American standards, it is played with a relatively minimal amount of actual snare drum technique—mostly single strokes, doubles and buzz roles—but as in playing the other instruments, the feel is everything. It is essential to articulate these simple patterns focusing on the feel. The *caixa* is also an integral part of the Escola de Samba.

Following is the basic framework for the snare. This basic pattern is further enhanced by buzz-strokes, rolls and other accents. The staccato notes are played by slightly accenting and pinching on the fulcrum of the stick with the thumb and index and middle fingers. *Think* short note and you'll get the right sound. The rolls are most commonly what I'll call a *sloppy* buzz stroke. It isn't played like a clean rudimental or orchestral roll. Basically accent and press the stick on the head to buzz. You can also try to play a shorter, staccato buzz strokes if you're playing continuous eighths, the tempo is fast and you're trying to buzz some of the eighths.

Following are some common patterns for samba. Keep in mind the instructions from the previous paragraph. The legato notes—the three consecutive rights—in patterns 2 and 5 are played by making one stroke for the first of the three rights and then just letting the other notes fall. This kind of slurs the three notes. This is also described in the *Tips* chapter. *The notes that have the sticking "RL" on one note are played as a two-handed buzz.*

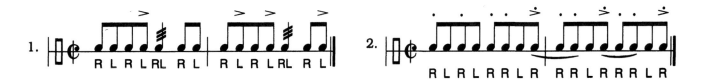

Following is a rhythm for the dance style called Maxixe. It also works very well for the Baiaó and some Marcha styles:

Pratos

Pratos is the name for cymbals. For an Escola, the most commonly used cymbals are a pair of hand-held crash cymbals with handles—similar to a pair of orchestral cymbals. They are most commonly used to accentuate downbeats with an occasional syncopation.

Following is the most common pattern. Many other syncopations are commonly played.

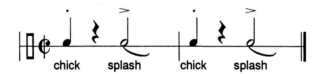

chick   splash   chick   splash

Repinique

Figure 1

Figure 2

The repinique, also called repique (*figure 1*), is a small double-headed drum played with a stick in one hand, with the other hand playing directly on the head (*figure 2*). It often serves as a sort of internal musical conductor in the Escola de Samba playing cues for the ensemble. It is used for solo fills, accentuations and rhythmic variations. It is also featured as a solo instrument, sometimes playing introductions to a Samba or soloing on a *Batucada*.

Due to the improvisational nature of the instrument, it is very hard to notate all of the rhythms played on it. Following is the basic timekeeping pattern. The rhythms played by the left hand can be muted strokes used as *filler*, open tones, or *slaps*.

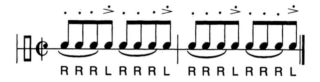

Here is the basic *call* used by the leader of the ensemble to start the samba:

Here are three common licks you can use as variations or solo fills. Number three is from the tamborim, but it works well here too.

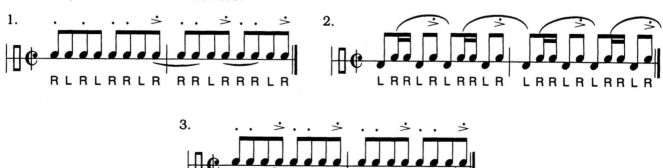

Caxixi

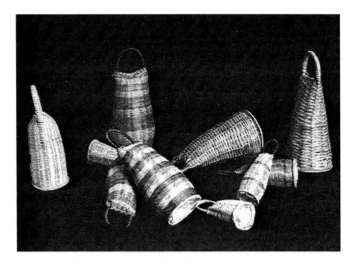

Figure 1

Figure 2

Caxixi are weaved baskets filled with either beads, sea shells, pebbles or beans. They have small handles on their tops. Being hand-weaved, there are many different shapes and sizes (*figure 1*). Originally, small caxixi were used with the *Berimbau* in *Capoeira* music. (More on the berimbau later.) Now they are used for rhythms or colorations in many styles. To create rhythmic patterns you can play one—or more—in each hand (*figure 2*). Following are some patterns. The top line is the right hand and the bottom the left.

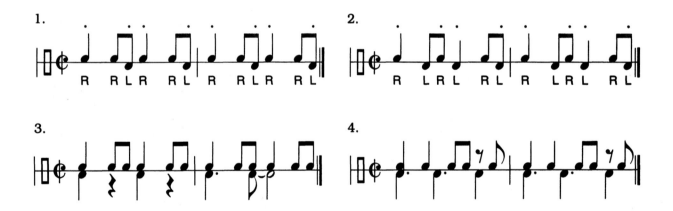

Following are odd meter combinations for the caxixi:

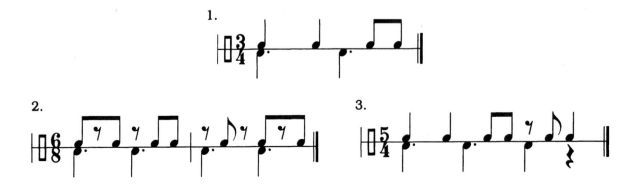

Berimbau

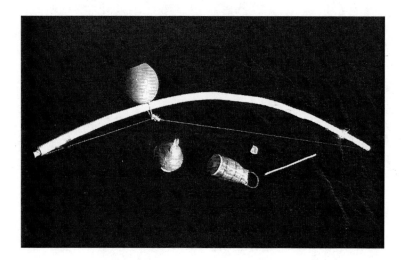

The Berimbau was brought to Brazil from Angola with the Capoeira music of the Bantú slaves. It is the instrument used to accompany this music. The Capoeira dance resembles the sparring in a martial art. Although it is like a depiction of a confrontation, its gracefulness resembles that of a ballet. *Capoeira* further evolved in the northern part of Brazil—in Bahia and other regions in the state of Pernambuco.

The instrument is made of a wooden arc—from a wood called *Biriba*—with a wire attached from end to end of the wooden arc forming the shape of an archer's bow. A round gourd with an opening on one side is attached to the lower, outside end of the bow, approximately 20 to 25 centimeters from the bottom, with a piece of cord. This functions as a resonator. The cord it is attached with is also tied around the wire. You pull on the cord to bend the pitch produced by the wire string. You alter the tone by pulling the gourd against and away from your body, thereby opening and closing the hole. The other three components are a coin or metal washer, which is held against the wire, a small stick to strike the wire and a small caxixi. (See illustrations on next page.) Although originally reserved strictly for use in Capoeira, it has found its way into other popular folk styles as well as other contemporary idioms. Some musicians have even recorded it as a solo instrument.

The many different sounds and nuances available on this instrument and the improvisational nature of the variations make it difficult to notate full playing. Following are some patterns to get you started. Begin by playing two bars of each pattern. Work these two bars into a groove and improvise with it by playing the two bars of the pattern and then two bars of improvised variations. Then take the next two bars and do the same. Next you can use the entire four bar patterns and play four bars of improvised variations. Finally, put it all together and improvise with that.

Here is a notation key for the basic strokes:

1. R.H.—*Notes on top of the line are strokes with the stick on the wire.*

2. R.H.—*Notes marked with* ◢ *indicate a caxixi stroke.*

3. L.H.—*Notes on the bottom line are notes indicating when to hold the coin against the wire.*

4. L.H.—*Notes marked with > mean to close the opening on the gourd by pulling it against your body.*

5. L.H.—*Notes marked with < mean to open the opening on the gourd by pushing it away from your body.*

The opening and closing of the hole on the gourd is largely a matter of the player's technical ability and musical taste. There is one common approach you can use at first. When the coin is not touching the wire play the notes closed. When the coin is touching play them open.

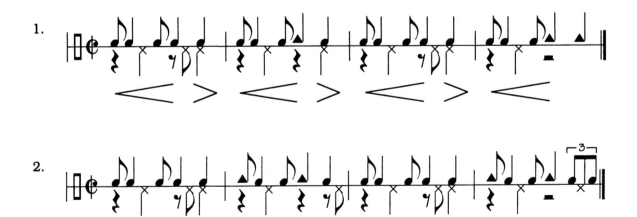

The Rhythm Section

Following are short examples of Brazilian melodies, bass lines, harmonies and comping patterns so you can familiarize yourself with how the rhythm section instruments work, and with some of the basic harmonic and melodic characteristics of these styles. You can practice with these examples by recording them into a sequencer and cutting and pasting until you have different vamps to play along with. If you don't have any MIDI gear, then record them to a tape and play along with that. If you don't have keyboard chops to play these examples yourself then ask a keyboard player friend to record them for you. It would also be very beneficial for you to develop some keyboard skills.

What the Bass Player Does

As a drummer/percussionist, one of your primary concerns should be what the bass player is playing and hooking up with it. Here are some basic patterns.

The first four examples are for Samba.

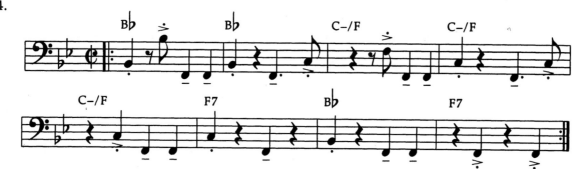

The next three examples are for the Samba De Partido Alto.

1.

2.

3.

The next two examples are for the Baiaó.

1.

2.

The next example is for the Frevo.

1.

The next two examples are for the Afoxé.

1.

2.

The next example is for the Bossa Nova.

1.

2.

Comping Patterns on the Piano and Guitar

The comping of the guitar or keyboard plays a major role in the groove and feel of the rhythm section. You should be also be familiar these instruments' patterns. Here are some approaches for the various styles.

The first two are for the Bossa on the guitar. Remember, this is a feature instrument of the Bossa, and the style was partially developed on the guitar.

1.

2.

The next two guitar examples are for the Samba (example 1) and Chorinho (example 2).

1.

2.

The next group of examples are for piano or keyboards.

Samba:

1.

2.

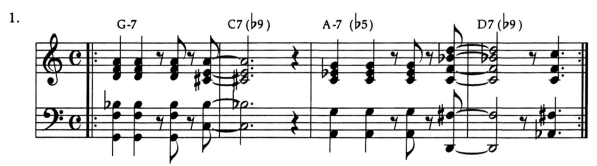

Bossa:

1.

Baião:

1.

2.

Frevo:

1.

Choro:

4.

On the following page is an example of a samba melody and rhythm section arrangement. It illustrates some common rhythm section interpretations of a Samba. The bass line—drawing from Bass Examples three and four—was used throughout, and the keyboard comping uses the pattern from Keyboard Example number two. Notice the offbeats in the turnarounds and how those relate to the patterns in the percussion and drum set examples. Try playing through the form using various approaches on both the drum set and with the percussion.

Summary

Having completed Part One of this book, you should now have a basic understanding of the origins and backgrounds of these rhythms and song-styles. You should also have some basic technical skills on the percussion instruments, and a wealth of rhythmic patterns to play in the various styles. Try to memorize as much of this material as you can, and listen to and learn as much music as you can in this style. This will be your ultimate guide for how to articulate these rhythms. In your listening try to identify and memorize things that you hear repeatedly—clichés. These typical phrases sometimes even identify a style, and many times are an indication of a player's real familiarity with a style. You can think of them as you would think of colloquialisms or slang in a language. You wouldn't want to apply them artificially anymore than you would want to speak in only slang terms, but they are an integral part of learning the idiomatic vocabulary of a style.

As you move on to the drum set, keep in mind that what is played on the drum set evolved from the percussion. The more you can apply from Part One, the more authentic you can sound.

One final point: I always encourage drum set players to learn more about percussion and percussionists to learn drum set. I also encourage both drummers and percussionists to learn more about harmony and melody and how the other instruments function—especially if you are really trying to learn a style and really trying to learn music. This will make your role as a musician much more significant for precisely this reason—you become a musician, not just a drummer. In Brazil, to belong to the Bateria of an Escola de Samba is to be part of an elite class. The same holds true in many Cuban and African cultures. In America, drummers tend to live with the stigma of just being the drummer. This stigma is disappearing because more drummers and percussionists are becoming total musicians. To play in an Escola you have to know many songstyles, rhythms and music in general—not just the beats. As was mentioned in the beginning of the book, there is a big difference between knowing the beats of a style and knowing the style. Knowing the style and music thoroughly can make you part of that elite class. Knowing just the beats insures that you will only be *just the drummer.*

Part II

Brazilian Drum Set

—— Rhythms ——
—— Songstyles ——
—— Techniques ——
—— Applications ——

Tips for Getting the Right Sound and Feel on the Drum Set

This material was covered in part one, but here it is again to refresh your memory. Keep in mind the three considerations for what type of sound you'll get when playing a percussion instrument. The first is the part of the stick you're playing with—the tip, the shoulder, or the butt end. The second is the type of stroke you use—an upstroke, downstroke, open stroke, dead–sticking stroke, accented, unaccented, loud, soft, or ghosted. The third is what part of the surface you strike. Virtually any part of any instrument can be played—not just the usual parts. Experiment with this. You may hear yourself playing sounds you've never played. This will greatly expand the range of sounds you get.

This information is particularly important for the drum set: it is very common in this style to dead–stick your ride patterns on the hi-hat or cymbals—not always, but it should be a technique you have under control. Using the shoulder of the stick on your ride will help get the right sound. The pictures below illustrate some hand positions for this. When you play on the drums use various stroke types—rim shots, buzzed notes, etc.. Ghosted notes are an essential part of getting the patterns to groove and feel right.

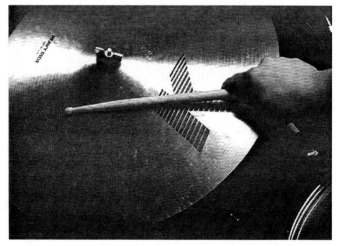

Also keep in mind that orchestrating your patterns on the drum set differently than you normally do can give you totally new grooves. Many times in these styles, the sticking patterns remain the same; you just move your hands to different sound sources and the feel changes completely. This seems obvious, but you'd be surprised at how many things you normally play where you may never have tried this.

Again, here are some common elements that run through these styles. Phrase to the last note of the bar—and the beat—whether in a time feel, fill, or in parts of solo phrases. This gives a feeling of forward motion to the groove—rather than playing the downbeats—which give a feeling of cadence to the time. Here are two examples:

1.

2.
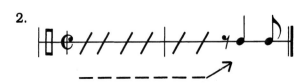

Here this is illustrated in two very common rhythmic phrases used in many Brazilian styles:

If you learn to stick the following phrase correctly, you will be very close to capturing the essence of the Samba rhythm. The key is to slur the three rights and pull back a little on the time.

Another common element in all Sambas is the short, unaccented note on the downbeat and the longer, heavier note on the upbeat of each bar.

Here are two rhythmic inflections common to the Baião, Afoxé, and other northern styles.

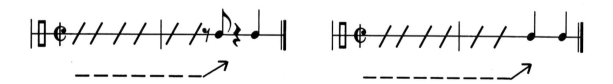

You should be able to articulate all of these inflections in all your time feels and improvisation on the drum set. Practice these by taking each phrase and building time feels, variations and improvisations around them.

Bossa Nova
Introduction

There are many theories regarding the evolution of the Bossa Nova. Some say the purpose was to cool down the Samba, others that it was a result of Brazilian musicians coming together with American Jazz artists and styles. While both of these are somewhat true, the cool down was more a result of the new compositional style, and the merging with Jazz took place after the style was recognized in Brazil—as well as somewhat internationally. You should note though, that the influence of Jazz was clear in the compositions and the instrumental improvisation of the leading developers of this style.

The Bossa evolved most directly from the style called *Samba Cançaó*—an extremely popular style of Samba in the 1940's and 50's. (The Samba section will tell you about this style.) In the 1950's the Samba Cançaó began to show influences from dance styles of other cultures—cha-cha, bolero, fox trots and others. Some younger musicians—mostly white, middle-class, as they were the ones responsible for the Samba Cançaó—were dissatisfied with this integration of styles, feeling it was deteriorating the quality of their music, and decided to make their own new style: Bossa Nova. Two musicians who had a big influence on the antecedent styles of the Bossa—particularly the Samba Cançaó—were Ary Barroso, the composer of many internationally recognized Brazilian pieces, and guitarist Noel Rosa. Pianist Johnny Alf influenced both players and writers in this style, and guitarist Garoto had a profound influence on all guitarists who played the Bossa. These individuals paved the way for the development of this new style.

Roughly translated the words Bossa Nova mean *new touch* or *new thing*. The lyric style is very subtle, and although a new, more syncopated way of playing the guitar developed, the instrumental accompaniment is also subtle and downplayed. While it maintains some of the rhythmic intensity of the Samba, the percussive accompaniment is less pronounced, more subdued. It is a style best suited for guitar and light percussion, with the vocals, lyrics and songwriting featured more prominently. In addition to the beautiful lyrics of the songs, the compositions feature very sophisticated harmonies and melodies that clearly showed European musical influence as well as the exposure to Jazz.

The musicians most well known for introducing the Bossa to the world are Antonio Carlos Jobim and Joaó Gilberto. Others include Luis Bonfa and Joaó Donato. Another significant development occurred through the merging of Brazilian composers and jazz instrumentalists such as Stan Getz and Charlie Byrd. These two American musicians, as well as several others, spent a great portion of their careers involved in collaborations with Brazilian musicians.

A technical note: A common misconception is that the Bossa is just a slow Samba. This is very much not the case. The two differ in all of the aspects just mentioned above, and in one more you can keep in mind for drum set performance. The Bossa is felt and articulated *in four*, while the Samba is *in two*. The time signature is not the issue. One is felt and played in four and the other in two. You can play both at the exact same tempo and they will feel and sound different. Listen to the recording for a comparison.

Bossa Nova in 4/4

Following is the basic Bossa Nova pattern for drum set. Work first with sticks in both hands. In the next section you'll work with brushes, and with the brush-stick technique. First get a nice smooth feel with your ride pattern on the hi-hat, along with the bass drum. Keep in mind the tips regarding riding with the shoulder of the stick, dead-sticking and playing on different parts of the surface you're riding on. These elements are an integral part of getting the right sound and feel. When this feels good, add the left hand on the rim of the snare. When you're comfortable playing this at a few different tempos move to the next section.

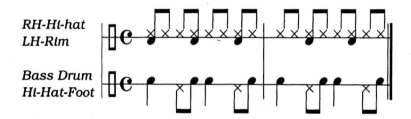

Following are some variations for the left hand. Substitute these patterns for the basic left hand pattern above. Always work in phrases—i.e.: two, four or eight times each pattern. Practice these at different tempos and dynamic levels. Also practice all the rhythms starting on the second bar of the pattern. There is no theoretical rule as to which position to play the patterns in. The rule is a musical one. You play the pattern in the way it sounds best with the melody and the entire composition. As stated in the tips section, playing time—*comping*—in Brazilian music is very much like playing jazz—you have the general patterns, and you play variations with them as dictated by the music. Don't perceive or learn patterns as being in a forward or reverse position. Learn the rhythms thoroughly and play the phrases the way the music tells you to. When you're comfortable move to the next section.

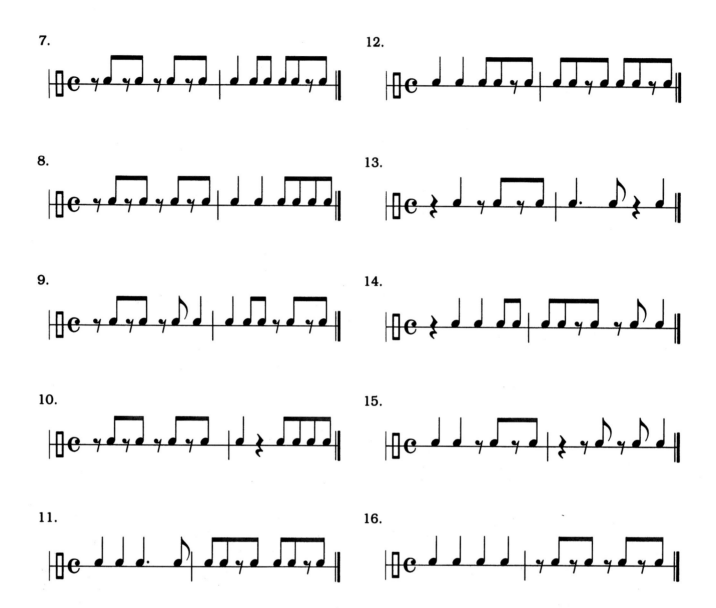

The number of patterns that can be played as variations are infinite. Improvise as much as you can to develop facility and to discover other ways to apply the rhythms. Again, always work in phrases. A good way to start is to take a two bar pattern and repeat it three times, then play a variation or a different pattern the fourth time. This gives you an eight bar phrase. If you now repeat this whole phrase again, and play a different variation the fourth time, you've got a sixteen bar phrase. In the performance of a song, you'll most likely use one or two basic patterns and some slight variations for most of the vocal and melody sections. During the improvisational sections you can generally mix things up a little more. Remember, the music should be your primary guide of what and how to play. Usually the leader, composer, arranger, and producer will also indicate what they have in mind. Always keep your ears and eyes open, be musical and be flexible.

Now that you have worked with this basic approach, go through all of the previous examples in the following ways:

1. Right hand on hi-hat—left hand on rim of snare (review).

2. Right hand on hi-hat—left hand on snare. *Use different stroke types on the snare, i.e.: rim shots, buzz strokes, dead strokes, etc.

3. Right hand on ride cymbal—left hand on rim of snare.

4. Right hand on ride cymbal—left hand on snare. Again, use a variety of sounds in your articulations.

5. Right hand on hi-hat, but now opening the hi-hat on the "1+" and "3+" of each bar—left hand on rim of snare. You can also play this as an accent only, without opening the hi-hat. When riding on the cymbal, try playing the accent on the bell with the shoulder of the stick. This is a common articulation in both Bossa and Samba.

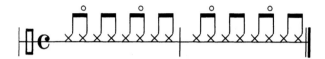

6. Same as #5 but with left hand on snare.

7. Right hand *sliding* eighth note time on the snare or floor tom with a brush—left hand on rim of snare (*figure 1*) with a stick. The second version of this is with the left hand directly on the snare (*figure 2*). (Later you'll also add other variations to the brush slides.) I play the slide in the following way—on the bottom, lower right of the snare. The arrows on the illustrations below indicate the position of brush for the eighth notes (*figures 3 and 4*). You can choose the way that is most comfortable for you. There are many ways to play this. Start by working on eighths first. You can think of the sound of the shaker. Also remember the little accent on "1+" and "3+".

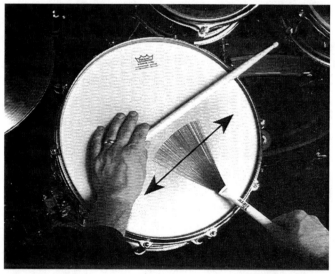

Figure 1

Figure 2

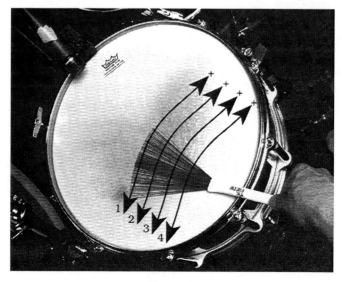

Figure 3

Figure 4

8. Same as #7 but with left hand on the snare.

9. Same as #8 but with brush in left hand.

10. Also with brushes, now try tap-sliding eighths in the right hand and sliding circles with the left hand (*figures 5 and 6*) You can use both full and half circles. As you get comfortable with this you can add accents and other articulations in each hand.

Figure 5

Figure 6

11. Working *with one hand at a time* (sticks and/or brushes), play constant eighths and accent the rhythms of the two bar phrases.

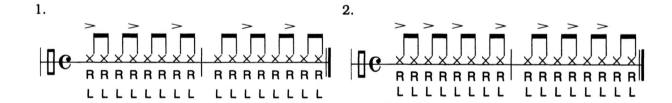

Once you have finished working with all of this material practice improvising with it as much as possible. You can move the left hand to other sound sources, add accents to the various voices for color, think about orchestrating the patterns in different ways on your drum kit, and practice going from one pattern to any other to create longer phrases. After doing this, add all of this material to things you already play and improvise with that. This is the way you will personalize the material. Again, *listen to and learn songs in this style.* There are some suggestions for listening at the end of the Bossa section. Practice playing *the music,* so you can learn to play Bossa Nova, not just a bunch of Bossa Nova patterns.

Keep in mind that the Bossa is derived from the Samba, so all of the rhythmic articulations and patterns from the Samba section can also be used for the Bossa. In essence the rhythms are the same. As mentioned earlier, the main difference is the feeling of four versus the feeling of two.

Bossa Nova in 5/4

The conceptual approach to playing the Bossa in odd time signatures is much the same as playing in 4/4. You should strive for the same smooth feel and use similar orchestrations. Following is a basic pattern for the drum set:

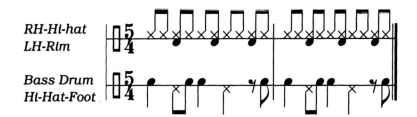

Once you feel comfortable with this, practice the following variations in the left hand. Start with the left hand on the rim. *The rhythms have not been beamed to denote a 2-3, 3-2 or 5 subdivision. You should practice and have control of all three versions.*

Now go back and apply all of the suggestions—1 through 11—from the Bossa in 4/4 section to all of the 5/4 patterns. You can repeat the one bar pattern alone, or combine two patterns to make a two bar phrase. Also try playing one pattern as a theme, and improvising the second bar. This will get you started playing longer phrases and will make you more comfortably in odd times.

Following are some different foot patterns you can try:

All of the left hand and right foot patterns are interchangeable and combinable. The right hand and the hi-hat can and should also be used for variations in the rhythms, as should the bass drum. They don't have to be restricted to ostinato patterns. It is sometimes desirable to have a sort of broken or linear time feel taking place between all four limbs—if the music calls for it.

Again, if you're not familiar or comfortable improvising variations or soloing with this feel, try using one of the one or two bar rhythmic patterns as a motif. Keep this as your theme, and practice improvising variations around it.

Bossa Nova in 6/4

The same approach as learning the Bossa in four is taken here.

Basic Pattern:

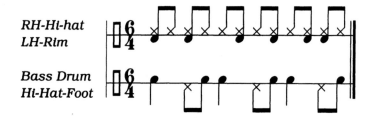

Here are some rhythmic variations for the left hand. As in the previous chapter, the notes were not beamed into subdivisions. You should practice phrasing in 6 (six equal beats in the measure), in half notes (measure divides in three), and in dotted half notes (measure divides in half).

1.

5.

2.

6.

3.

7.

4.

8.

Bossa Nova in 7/4

Once again, follow the same approach as for the Bossa in four. Go through all of the previous instructions and you'll learn the feels thoroughly. Here is a basic framework to start with:

RH-Hi-hat
LH-Rim

Bass Drum
Hi-Hat-Foot

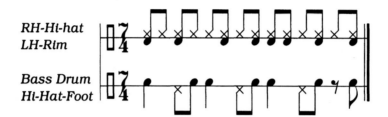

Here are some variations. The subdivisions can be in 7, in 4-3 or in 3-4. Practice them all.

1.

2.

3.

Significant Artists and Suggested Listening
Bossa Nova

Following is a list of artists who made significant contributions to the development of the Bossa. These are composers and instrumentalists renowned for their work in this idiom. The purpose of the list is to aid in you becoming familiar with important musicians of this style. In building a library of this style you can look for recordings by these artists or with contributions from them.

Vinicius de Moraes
—Poet, author, diplomat, lyricist. Wrote lyrics for over 200 songs. Was an important figure in the linking of the Samba-Cançaó and the Bossa Nova. Collaborated extensively with Jobim and other key Bossa Nova artists.

Ary Barroso
—Composer of Aquarela do Brasil as well as many internationally recognized Brazilian pieces. Collaborated extensively with other composers. His compositions were recorded by many Brazilian as well as American artists.

Garoto
—Guitarist who influenced the guitar style of the Bossa with his harmonic approaches to Samba and Choro styles.

Noel Rosa
—Guitarist with major influence on the styles that led to the Bossa Nova.

Antonio Carlos Jobim ("Tom" Jobim)
—Composer, guitarist, vocalist. Internationally renowned and innovative composer of many of the most well-known Bossa Novas.

Johnny Alf
—Composer and pianist who had a large impact on the Bossa composers and instrumentalists.

Joaó Gilberto
—Guitarist and vocalist who in 1958/59 brought the Bossa to international attention with his recording and performance of *Desafinado* by Jobim. One of the originators of the new Bossa guitar style of that period.

Joaó Donato
—Pianist and composer who's contributions to the Bossa included much American jazz influence.

Luiz Bonfa
—Guitarist and composer of many pieces that influenced the developing Bossa style.

Astrud Gilberto
—Vocalist who's duet rendition (with her husband Joaó Gilberto) of *Garota de Ipanema (Girl From Ipanema)* with both Portuguese and English lyrics brought her international recognition as a Bossa stylist.

Carlos Lyra
—Guitarist and composer of many Bossa standards. Formed a guitar academy in Rio with Roberto Menescal, to work with progressive Bossa Nova guitar styles.

Roberto Menescal
—Guitarist and composer of many well known Bossas.

Nara Leaó
—Vocalist and Bossa Nova stylist who recorded many famous Bossa compositions. She was a key vocalist and figure in the 1964 Brazilian political protest musical *Opiñaó.*

Oscar Castro-Neves—
—Guitarist and composer of many early Bossas.

Edu Lobo
—Guitarist and songwriter of many pieces in the early sixties. Known for lyrics that were politically tinged.

Baden Powell
—Influential guitarist who recorded many Bossas as well as other Brazilian styles. His guitar playing and improvisation included much Afro-Brazilian as well as jazz influence.

Newton Mendoça
—Pianist and composer who collaborated with Jobim on many now-famous Bossas.

Aloysio de Olivera
—Composer and collaborator of many Bossa standards. As director for the *Odeon* record label, was in part responsible for the release of Joaó Gilberto's *Chega de Saudade* single which is considered by some to be the first Bossa recording.

Sergio Mendes
—Composer and leader of the *Sexteto Bossa Rio,* an early Bossa group in Rio. He later collaborated with many American Jazz artists in Brazil and gained most of his recognition through his leading of various Brazilian groups in the United States from the group *Brazil '66* to current releases.

Elizeth Cardoza
—Vocalist . Her album *Cançaó do Amor Demais* featured Joaó Gilberto playing guitar. This was one of the first Bossa recordings.

Marcos Valle
—Composer whose Bossa music included lyrics of social commentary and political criticism.

Ronaldo Bóscoli
—Composer/songwriter. Wrote lyrics for the Roberto Menescal song *Rio.*

Luis Eça
—Influential pianist, composer/ songwriter and arranger of many popular bossa novas. Arranger of Milton Nascimentos first album. Performer in many Brazilian styles.

Here is a list of compositions that are considered to be Bossa Nova standards. You should learn as many of these tunes as possible, and you should familiarize yourself with many renditions of each particular song.

By: ***Antonio Carlos Jobim:***
*With Vinicius de Moraes
**With Newton Mendoça
***With Aloysio de Oliveira

Chega de Saudade*
Desafinado**
Triste
If You Never Come to Me
Corcovado
Wave
Aguas de Março
Luiza
Ela é Carioca
Garota de Ipanema*
Água de Beber*
O Grande Amor*
Só Danço Samba*
Insensatez*
Meditaçáo**
Samba de Uma Nota Só
A Felicidade*
Samba do Aviaó
Vivo Sonhando
Por Toda Minha Vida*
Dindi***
Demais***
Eu e o Amor*
Se Todos Fossem Iguais a Vocé

By: ***Luiz Bonfa:***

Manha de Carnaval
A Chiuva Caiu
Engano

By: ***Joaó Gilberto***

Bim Bom

By: ***Baden Powell***

Samba Triste (Sad Samba)

By: ***Carlos Lyra***
*With Ronaldo Bóscoli
**With Vinicius de Moraes
***With Newton Mendoça
****With Aloysio de Oliveira

Maria Ninguém
Saudade Fez um Samba*
Lobo Bobo*
Coisa Mais Linda**
Samba do Carioca**
Primavera**
Sabe Voce**

By: ***Joaó Donato***

Minha Saudade

By: ***Marcos Valle*** and ***Paul Sergio Valle***

Samba de Veraó (Summer Samba)
Lágrima Flor

By: ***Ronaldo Bóscoli*** and ***Roberto Menescal***

O Barquinho (Little Boat)
Rio
Vocé
Telefone
A Volta
Nós e o Mar

By: ***Vinicius de Moraes*** and ***Toquinho***

Aquarela
As Cores de Abril

Samba
Introduction

Before beginning this section, go back and review the Samba section in part one. Review the rhythmic patterns of each of the percussion instruments, and the basic characteristics of various Samba styles. Also review all of the *tips* section. It is important to keep in mind that most aspects of drum set playing in this style were derived from the rhythms of one, or several, of the percussion instruments. There are many different samba styles and many ways to play each of them, and the particular type of ensemble you're playing in will determine what you will play. Remember that regardless of the song-style or the tempo, the samba is always felt and played *in two*. The foundation or bass rhythm for the samba is basically the downbeats of the bar—in cut time the *one* and the *two*—with the accentuation on the two. This rhythm is played on the surdo, the bass drum of the Samba. The general phrasing to the last note of the bar, and the use of traditional Brazilian rhythmic vocabulary will make your playing sound more authentic. Adapting the techniques and rhythms of the percussion instruments to the drum set will enhance your playing in this style tremendously. Also keep in mind that all of the music being presented here is folkloric in nature. It originated and was first played by the common folk in the streets—much like the origin of the blues in the United States. These players were not necessarily musicians with tremendous technique on any instrument, and if they were it was more happenstance than a conscious effort. As a matter of fact the instruments themselves were very primitive by our standards. Technique on your instrument is a big part of our focus in music today. Just don't make your main focus a technical one. Your main priority should be to capture the feel. The technical concerns should be secondary—assuming you already have your chops together. If you don't, then you must address this before you can approach this study musically. On the following page is a percussion score for a basic *Batucada* for you to review.

Samba Percussion Score

Here is a basic score of the *Bateria* of an Escola de Samba to refresh your memory about the percussion parts. These are only basic structures and many variations can be played on each instrument. Sometimes the variations themselves define a particular style of Samba. Within certain styles the role of some instruments involves a great deal of improvisation and variations of the basic pattern. All of this should be applied to your drum set playing. (Refer back to Part I for more specific information on each instrument.)

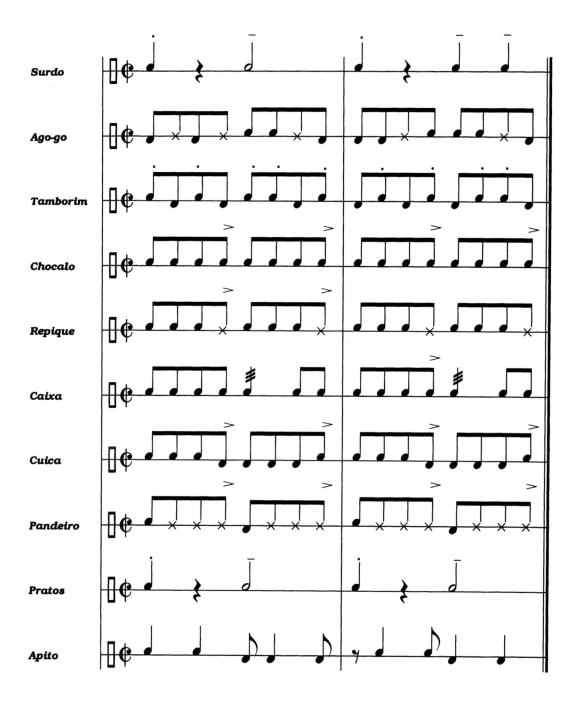

Basic Drum Set Approaches

Following is the first set of rhythms for playing Samba styles on the drum set. There are many ways to apply them, so don't just play them as written and stop there. Learn this and all other material available, and listen to as much of this style as possible. Keep improvising and mixing things up until the material becomes your own.

Begin by working with the following foot patterns first. If you have played Samba before, chances are you are familiar with foot pattern #1. Unfortunately many drummers are only aware of this one foot pattern. Patterns #2 and #3 will actually give you the most traditional sound because they most closely emulate the *Surdo* and *Pratos*. Pattern #4 emphasizes the upbeat by placing an eighth note before it, but not before the downbeat. All will give you a distinctly different flavor in the feel. When you use each will depend on the musical context you find yourself in at any given time. Work with all of them in order to build your repertoire of Samba playing. To get started, pick the pattern you're most comfortable with, and go on to the following exercises. Then come back and do the whole sequence again until you've covered all the foot patterns.

Six Foot Patterns:
The top line is the hi-hat and the bottom line the bass drum. The staccato and accent markings in examples 1 and 5 indicate the long and short notes of the surdo rhythm and the samba. Try to make your downbeat a little more pointed and less accented than the upbeat. Think short-long. Not all compositions will call for this. Sometimes it may be more desirable to play it without long-short articulation .

1.
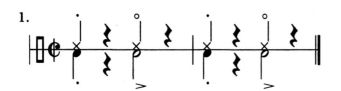

4.

2.
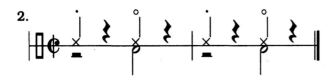

5.

3.
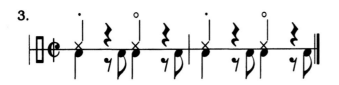

6.
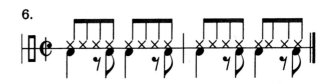

7.

Practice the following patterns with *both hands in unison—cymbal and snare*—over all of the above foot patterns. There are two reasons for this approach. The first: because this is actually one way that you play Samba on the drum set. The other is more technical. Many drummers are under the impression that playing Latin rhythms on the drum set involves playing very busy, syncopated patterns with the hands over a foot ostinato. While to an unfamiliar ear it may sound like a lot is going on with the hands over a foot pattern, just the opposite is more often the case. What is actually going on in each limb is very simple. It is where each rhythm is placed and the overall rhythmic interpretation that creates the intense syncopated feeling. By working with your hands in unison, you're not only learning actual ways of playing Samba, but you can focus on how the rhythms line up between your limbs. You will immediately be able to hear if you are out of sync between your hands and feet and make an adjustment. It also makes for a great technical workout.

Begin by playing one foot pattern at a time and playing all of the two bar phrases over it. Repeat each phrase at least twice or four times so that you're working with four or eight bar phrases. Move from one to the next without stopping. Practice until you can move from one pattern to any other without stopping. Focus on the feel in your articulation of the rhythms, and also try to focus on your overall groove. Once you're past the technical elements practice improvising.

Suggestions for Variations and Improvisation

Now practice playing all of the two bar patterns you just learned with the following suggestions.

1. Practice playing in four bar phrases by playing two bars of a theme or *fixed* pattern—using one of the given phrases—and two bars of improvised variations. Following is an example. Use the other patterns you just learned and make up variations like this. This is a great way to work on your phrasing.

Theme Pattern: *Improvise Variations:*

2. Practice eight bar phrases by using a four bar theme pattern—made up of one of the given two bar phrases *repeated*—and four bars of improvised variations.

Theme pattern:

Improvise Variations:

3. Practice eight bar phrases by using a two bar theme pattern *repeated three times*, and a two bar improvised variation at the end.

Theme Patterns:

Improvise Variations:

4. Sixteen bar phrases can be made by repeating two eight bar phrases with variations at the end of each of the eight bar phrases.

5. Thirty-two bar phrases can be made up of two groups of eight—making sixteen—and then repeating the whole thing again with another variation at the end of the second sixteen.

What's being driven at here is that it is essential to develop a strong sense of phrasing. You must repeat things and then develop variations in order to play good strong phrases. *Don't play lots of variations and no theme.* Your playing will sound very disjunct, and your listeners won't have any idea what you're playing. Remember, in Brazilian music it is the melody that will dictate what will be played. Learn tunes and practice singing a tune and improvising the drum set parts around the melody.

Once you can play phrases with the previous suggestions, begin working with the following exercises. Apply all of the previous phrasing suggestions as you learn each new technique.

1. Play all phrases hands in unison, cymbal and snare, over all six patterns. (Review.)

2. Play all phrases on the snare with the right hand, and *fill in* the missing eighth notes with the left hand. Do this two ways: first with the left hand *filling in* on the snare; second, *filling in* on the hi-hat. Then mix it up. Your left hand notes should be ghosted.

This pattern;

R.H.
L.H.

Becomes:

3. Practice improvising with the above two techniques applying all of the phrasing suggestions.

4. Play constant eight notes—*sticking RLRL RLRL*—and *buzz* all the rhythms of the two bar phrases. Following is an example of this using rhythmic figure number one from the previous section. *These are short staccato buzz strokes.*

This:

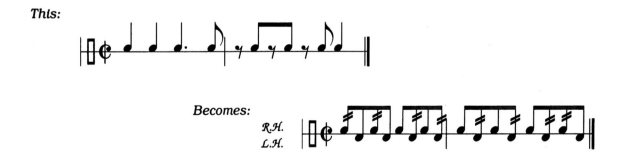

R.H.
L.H.

Becomes:

5. Play constant eighth notes buzzing every stroke and accenting the rhythms of the two bar phrases. Playing patterns like this is an offshoot of the Samba snare drum part played in Escolas de Samba, as well as a variation of the Maxixe rhythm.

The following approach introduces the use of ostinatos for the ride pattern. You'll work first with the following six ostinatos. Although you have only six rhythmic patterns, the use of accents, hi-hat openings on the accented notes, or playing the accented notes on the bell of the cymbal with the shoulder of the stick, give you many variations.

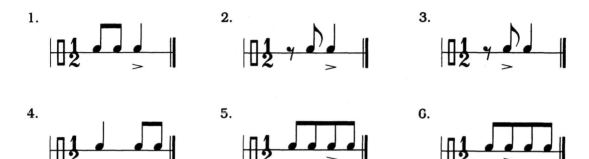

Go through the ostinatos as follows:

1. Right hand on closed hi-hat. Left hand plays the two bar phrases from the previous section.

2. Right hand on hi-hat opening the accented notes. Left hand plays the two bar phrases.

3. Right hand on ride cymbal, left hand plays the phrases.

4. Right hand on cymbal with accented notes on the bell with the shoulder of the stick.
   Left hand plays the phrases.

Play the following two-handed combinations. Notice the left hand is filling in the missing note of a three note ostinato. The lefts can be played ghosted, slightly dragged or slurred, or accented. Number one is the most common samba permutation.

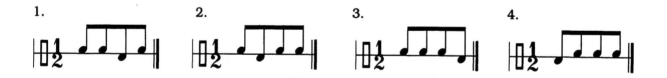

Now try doubling the left hand note. This layers two notes and creates a nice feel.

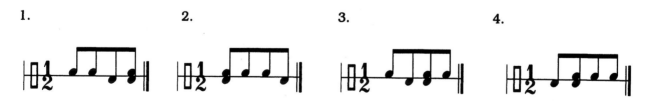

Orchestrate all of these examples on different sound sources on the drum set. Think of the percussion instruments' sounds and patterns.

Sticking Combinations

Following are some sticking combinations that work particularly well for Samba. Remember, that you must have accented and unaccented—*ghosted*—notes to get the right feel. You can use the stickings to develop time feels, variations, and improvisation.

This first one uses the inverted paradiddle combination RLLR LRRL. Practice both accent possibilities written here. Example three is one possible orchestration of this sticking around the set.

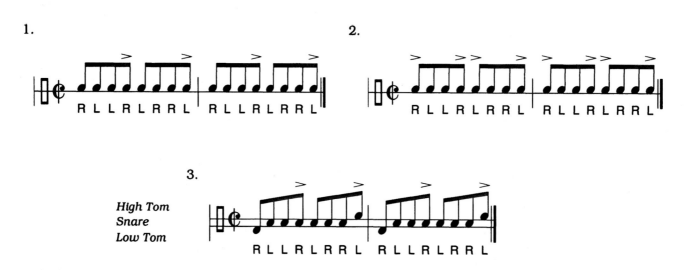

The next example is another paradiddle combination, RRLR LLRL. Again, observe the accents and ghosted notes. Orchestrate it into some patterns that are useful for you.

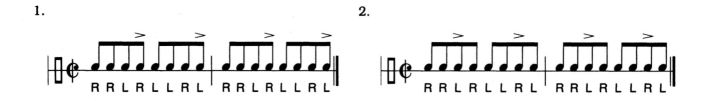

This combination, RLL or LRR, is good for displacing a single accent every three beats. It is useful for variations in your timekeeping patterns or improvisation.

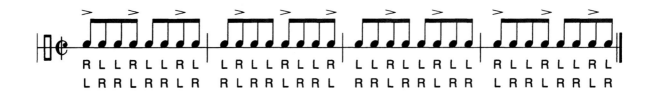

Like the three note sticking in the previous example, this five note sticking: RLRLL or LRLRR, gives you yet another accent displacement. You can also try a regular five stroke roll sticking, RLLRR LRRLL. Work these into different combinations around the set.

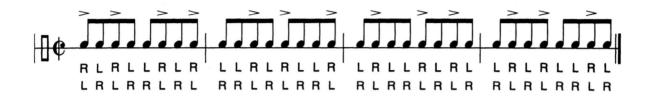

R L R L L R L R   L L R L R L L R   L R L L R L R L   L R L R L L R L
L R L R R L R L   R R L R L R R L   R L R R L R L R   R L R L R R L R

The following stickings can be looked at a couple of different ways. They are an extension of a previous exercise you did, in which you took the two bar Samba patterns in one hand, and filled in the missing eighths with your other hand. These three examples use the sticking RLRLRLL or LRLRLRR as their base. Since this is a seven note sticking and you're playing in two (or four), you can add whatever notes you need to round out the phrase. You can also do this with the previous two examples. Another thing you can try is to bring out only the right hand, or only the left hand accents. You'll be surprised at the different rhythmic patterns you can come up with. You don't have to limit yourself to only right or only left hand accents. Think of the overall rhythmic pattern. Keep the Samba phrases in mind to maintain an idiomatic sound. For improvisation, the combinations are limitless. The first two examples bring out the accents that fall in the right hand. The third brings out the left hand. I strongly recommend you study the *Patterns II* book by *Gary Chaffee* for an extensive look at sticking possibilities. While your at it I'd suggest you study *Patterns I* and *Patterns III* also. You can apply all of that material directly to these interpretations.

1.

R L R L R L L R   L R L R L L R L   R L R L L R L R   L R L L R L R L
L R L R L R R L   R L R L R R L R   L R L R R L R L   R L R R L R L R

R L R L R L L R   L R L R L L R L   R L R L L R L R   L R L L R L R L
L R L R L R R L   R L R L R R L R   L R L R R L R L   R L R R L R L R

2.

3.

You should also work with stickings that contain flams. Use the standard rudiment repertoire and also try making up sticking combinations of your own.

Samba with Brushes

Playing Samba with brushes, like playing any style with them, is an art in itself. There are a few basic concepts that relate to playing brushes in any style that you should have down first. The basic technique of playing brushes involves sliding rhythms and sticking rhythms. The sliding patterns can take many different shapes. You can slide straight lines left to right or back and forth, you can slide circles, half circles, or any number of combinations. In this sliding you have to be able to do three things. One is to articulate various rhythms to generate a time feel, the second is to create a sound texture, and three, articulate accents in those slides to embellish the time feels. Following are a few suggestions and technical exercises that you can work on to build up some chops with the brushes.

1. Practice all of the sticking exercises you practice with sticks—Rudiments, Stick Control, etc.—with brushes. This will get you comfortable with the feel of the brushes in your hands. It'll also be great for your chops in general.

2. **Sliding exercise A**: Practice one hand at a time. Figures 1 and 2 show the right hand, 3 and 4 show the left. Slide the brush on the snare as is shown in the illustration below. Keep some simple time with your feet. At each of the *end points* of the slide you will articulating —by means of a slight accent—a rhythmic scale going from half notes to thirty-seconds and back down again. The first couple of rhythms are illustrated:

Figure 1

Figure 2

Figure 3

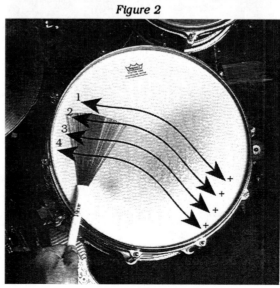

Figure 4

3. ***Sliding exercise B***: Again, practice one hand at a time. Slide circles like the illustration shows. Figure 5 shows the left hand and figure 6 the right. Focus at the top of the circle. This is the point at which you'll make your rhythmic inflection (indicated by the arrow). Practice articulating the rhythmic scale as stated in number two above. As you articulate faster rhythms the circles will get smaller. Half note circles would be your largest circle and would get progressively smaller as the rhythmic rate increases from eighth notes to triplets to sixteenths and faster. As you slow down the rhythmic rate the circles get larger.

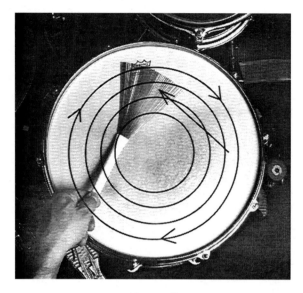
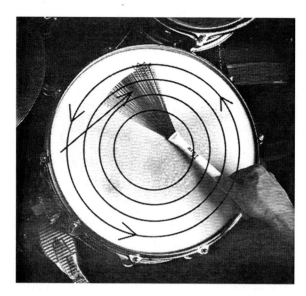

Figure 5   *Figure 6*

4. ***Sliding exercise C***: Do the same as *Sliding exercise B* except instead of articulating the rhythmic scale, work on specific note values one at a time. Articulate two notes per bar, three notes, four notes per bar, quarter note triplets starting on and off the beat. For example, in working on four notes per bar you can accent four quarters on the downbeats, four eighths on the upbeats, four eighths as the last eighth of a triplet and so on. As the illustration show, slide circles and practice making the rhythmic inflection at the top of the circle shown by the arrow. You can also do these two exercises with the rhythmic accent at the bottom of the circle as you make the sweep upward.

5. Take pages five through seven of the Stick Control book (by: George Lawrence Stone), and instead of sticking the combinations, play the stickings by sliding them. Articulate the rhythmic accent at the downward point of the slide as indicated by the arrow (*figure 7*). The brush will make sound as it slides back up but it should be less pronounced than the downward strokes. This gives you varying textures. The up and down slides work like accented and ghosted notes.

                     RLRL RLRL
                     LRLR LRLR
                     RRLL RRLL
                     LLRR LLRR
                     RLRR LRLL
                     RLLR LRRL

Figure 7

Once you've practiced the above, the next step is to put the hands together to create time feels in whatever style you're playing—in this case Samba. If you've practiced all of the suggested exercises, the rest should come relatively easily. Following are some approaches to playing the Samba with brushes:

1. Slide eighths with one hand and play the twenty-two two bar rhythms from the *Samba: Basic Drum Set Approaches* section with the other hand. Tap the rhythms with the left hand brush while the right continues sliding the eighths.

2. Slide eighths by alternating hands—right, left, right left—and play the rhythms from the same samba section mentioned above as accented slides. Articulate the accent in the slide, in whatever hand it falls on in the alternating eighths. Exercise #5 will help this a lot.

3. Improvise with a combination of the above two methods and then incorporate all of the rhythmic patterns covered so far. Most players develop a pretty personal technique with brushes. There is no standard method. Practice these examples, listen, and copy everything you see and hear. As you start getting these techniques under control, you'll begin to develop your own approach.

It may be hard to understand these concepts from the written explanations. Listen to the recorded examples and try to imitate the sound and feel. You should also work with a teacher and/or an educational video so you can see these examples played.

Brush-Stick Technique

Although the brush-stick approach originated on the drum set, there are direct connections to certain sounds and techniques of various percussion instruments. First, several instruments such as the *Repinique* and the *Tamborim* are played with a stick in one hand and the other (bare) hand playing assorted notes directly on the head. The brush–stick method somewhat emulates that approach. Secondly, the sound of the brush sliding closely resembles the sound of the *Chocalo* (shaker).

The notation reads as follows:

Top line is right hand, bottom line is left hand.

The left hand holds the brush and the right hand holds the stick (figure 1).
(Do the reverse if you are left-handed.)

On all beats notated with an "X" play the stick on the brush (figure 2).

Between the stick playing on the brush, the brush muting the head, and the various brush and stick strokes you can make (rim shots, brush sweeps, flams, etc.), you have a wide variety of sounds available, so improvise and experiment.

Figure 1

Figure 2

On the following page are three patterns to start with.

1.

2.

3.

When you're comfortable with these patterns practice them as follows;

1. Play these over all six foot patterns.

2. Move hands to different sound sources.

3. Play with brushes in both hands.

4. Try to combine *tap* strokes with *slide* strokes on the brushes.

5. Play the *filling in* exercise from the *Samba—Suggestions for Variations and Improvisation* section. The *filled in* notes will now be with the brush. Improvise and experiment with different stick strokes playing on the brush as well as with other stroke types and variations.

6. Listen to the audio examples of this and other recorded examples. Improvise to develop your own versions.

The next two pictures indicate another way to play Samba with the Brush-Stick technique. The right hand slides eighth notes (as well as improvising variations), and the left hand plays rhythms on either the rim (*figure 3*), or directly on the snare (*figure 4*).

Figure 3

Figure 4

Batucada

As mentioned in Part One, a *Batucada* is a Samba played with only percussion. In an Escola de Samba, this would mean the singers and the *Cavaquinho* would not play and only the percussion would be featured. With the *Bateria* of an Escola numbering three to five hundred percussionists, you can imagine this is a pretty powerful sound.

In a group (band) setting this would mean the drums—and percussion, if present—would play alone. If you are playing drum set with a percussionist present, then you would cover the Surdo and Caixa (snare drum) parts, and the bass drum and hi-hat. If there is no percussion then you still need to cover the Surdo and Caixa, but any other percussion you have on your set that you can add to your patterns would only enhance the feel, making it more authentic. Some very easy things to mount are Ago-go bells and Tamborims.

Following are some frameworks for playing the Batucada or *Samba de Carnaval,* as it's sometimes called. These are only basic frameworks. The basic structure starts with a simplified Caixa part and the two surdos. You can elaborate quite a bit on the melody between the high and low Surdos—your high and low toms. Remember there are three Surdo parts you can draw from. Playing the accents and ghosted notes are essential for the right feel.

The first example is your starting point—the snare drum with the low Surdo part.
* *Use your floor tom for the Surdo notes.*

This second example incorporates the high surdo into a basic pattern.
* *Use your high and low toms for the two surdo parts.*

These next examples elaborate a little more on the Surdo parts and the accents. If you have more than one nounted tom or two floor toms or a tom on your hi-hat side, incorporate them into the patterns.

1.

2.

3.

4.

5.

6.

Now that you have some material under your belt, start putting these patterns together and improvise longer phrases. Following are some ideas to get you started. Notice how the phrases are built employing the concepts stated in the *Samba: Suggestions For Improvisation* section: *longer phrases are built through the repetition and grouping of shorter phrases and slight variations.*

Four bar phrases made by combining material from the two bar phrase and adding variations.

1.

2.

Eight bar phrases made by combining material from the two and four bar phrases and adding variations.

3.

4.
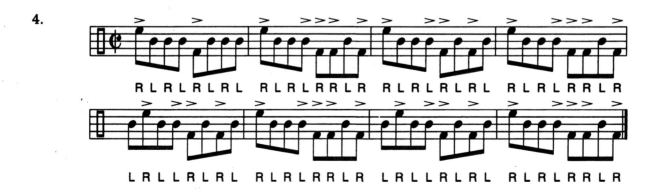

Samba Cruzado

The word *cruzado* literally means crossed in Portuguese. Hence *Samba Cruzado* means crossed Samba. The crossed refers to your arms being crossed at the drum set. Your left hand crosses over your right and plays the Surdo parts, while your right hand plays various Samba phrases on the snare drum (*figures 1 & 2*). (*Figure 3 on the next page shows a close-up of the hand position for playing the short, muted note of the surdo pattern. The index finger helps keep the stick against the head since your other hand is not free to mute the drum.*) This approach might have developed in part because most people are right handed. Most of the improvising in these patterns is done with one hand on the snare while the other plays the Surdo ostinatos on the toms. Since Brazilian drum set players are generally not as technically oriented as American drummers this approach may have evolved in part to allow the strong hand to do the improvising. (This is just a theory and is not a historical fact.) You should first practice these patterns with the traditional *cruzado* approach. Then you should reverse the hands and play all the Surdo parts with the right hand and improvise with the left hand. You can also put a floor tom on the left side of your set, and play the patterns of the Surdo in the left hand. The improvisation will still be in the right, but your hands won't be crossed.

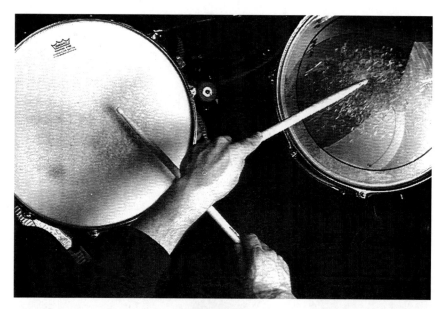

Figure 1

Figure 2

107

Figure 3

First, work on playing the following Surdo patterns. You can practice this with the left hand now, do all the patterns *cruzado*, then work on the opposite. Or you can practice the Surdo with both hands now. The Surdo pattern on a single drum is played with one hand, by playing a *dead–stroke* on the downbeat, and an open stroke on the upbeat.

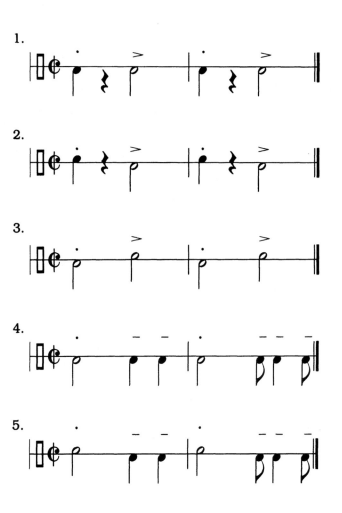

Once you're comfortable playing the Surdo part with one hand, add the snare drum. First work with repeating a two bar phrase. When you have a good groove happening, you can begin improvising variations.

These are two very common phrases:

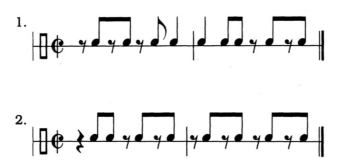

Here are some more common phrases. Also, go back and play all the two bar patterns from the first Samba section. Combine all the two bar phrases with all of the Surdo patterns.

If you have trouble putting the two parts together you can write one under the other so you can see where the hands play together and apart. Snare pattern 1 above with Surdo pattern 4 from the previous page would look like this:

Samba Marcha

The Samba Marcha was derived from a combination of various Samba styles and the Portuguese military parades. It initially evolved through adapting the rhythms of the parade snare drum to the Samba groove. The Samba Marcha is played at slow to medium tempos. You'll be working primarily with snare and Surdo patterns.

Following is a basic pattern. Notice the snare pattern is the same as the basic pattern from the percussion score of an Escola de Samba. You're playing a scaled down Surdo part on the floor tom. The roll on beat three is done as a one handed buzz while the right hand plays the floor tom simultaneously. This is only a skeleton pattern. There are many variations that can be played.

Another way to play the Samba Marcha is to play the snare pattern with only one hand. Then play phrases on two toms or mounted percussion instruments with the other hand. (*Some examples of phrases are on the next page.*) If you play the snare with the right hand, you'll have to cross over your right arm with your left. You'll be playing *cruzado*. This is the traditional way to do this. You can do it both ways.

Start by practicing the snare drum part with your right hand. When you're comfortable work with phrases in the left hand. This requires a bit of coordination, so don't get discouraged if you can't do it right away. Try this rhythm with different foot patterns and finally, work on improvising with the left hand.

Play the following pattern on the snare with your right hand. When you're comfortable, add the left hand parts.

Play the following patterns with the left hand on your toms or ago–go bells:

1.

2.

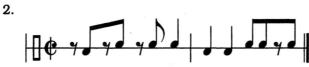

3.

For more combinations, continue the snare part with the one hand, and go back to the two bar Samba phrases from the *Basic Drum Set Approaches* section. Take the two bar phrases and improvise, breaking them up between two toms. Improvise accents and orchestrations on your set.

If you're having trouble playing these combinations, it may help to see the two parts together—one on top of the other—as we did with the Batucada examples. This way it's easier to see when the hands fall together and apart. Here are the previous two examples notated like that.

1.

R.H.

L.H.

2.

R.H.

L.H.

Samba de Partido Alto

Many Samba rhythm styles have only very subtle differences between them in the percussion rhythms and instrumentation. Many times, the percussion stays more or less the same, and it's the harmony, lyric style, or the region that a Samba emanates from that determines its identity and name. Not all Samba styles are like this though. The Partido Alto is a style that has big differences in both its lyric approach *and* its rhythms.

In the vocal area, this style features short repeated chorus passages that the ensemble singers answer with improvised verses. At the point of its development, many Sambas featured long vocal passages with no improvisation.

In the rhythmic area, it contains some syncopated rhythm patterns that the other Samba styles do not—the most prevalent of these being the strong accent off of the first beat, and the accent on the *and* of beat three. These are marked mostly by the pandeiro, the cuica, and the tamborim. The snare part is also different than in most other Carnaval Sambas. Although in a simple Partido Alto the Surdo still marks the downbeats, it also often plays the other syncopations and rhythmic lines. Following is a score illustrating a basic Partido Alto for percussion.

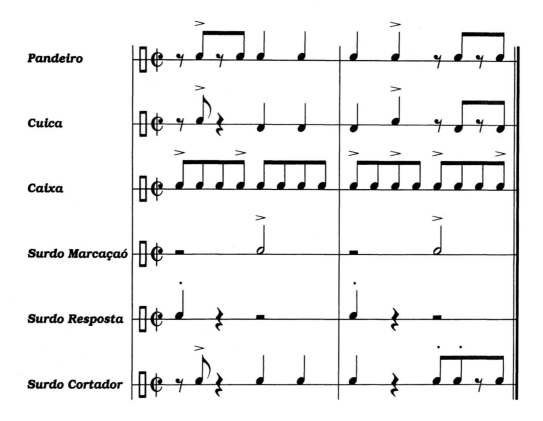

Following is the most common way to play this rhythm on the drum set. The pattern can also be played starting with the second bar of the phrase. Remember that you don't think of this as forward or reverse. Play according to how it sounds best with the melody and the rhythm section arrangement. For all the following examples the top line marked "X" is the hi-hat and the bottom line is snare and bass drum. Instructions for other combinations and variations follow the examples.

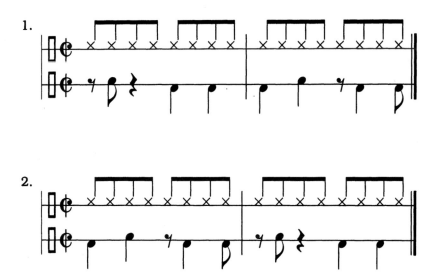

Here is a common variation. It is also notated in both positions.

Now practice improvising variations. This rhythm lends itself to a lot of funk-style interpretations, so think of this factor too as you're coming up with grooves. There are some variations on the following page. In an arrangement of a contemporary song it is very common for one part of the song to be Partido Alto and another to be a regular samba groove. Practice going back and forth between the two types of rhythms. It is very important to be able to go back and forth smoothly, as well as set up the two feels with fills and variations.

Here are a few more combinations.

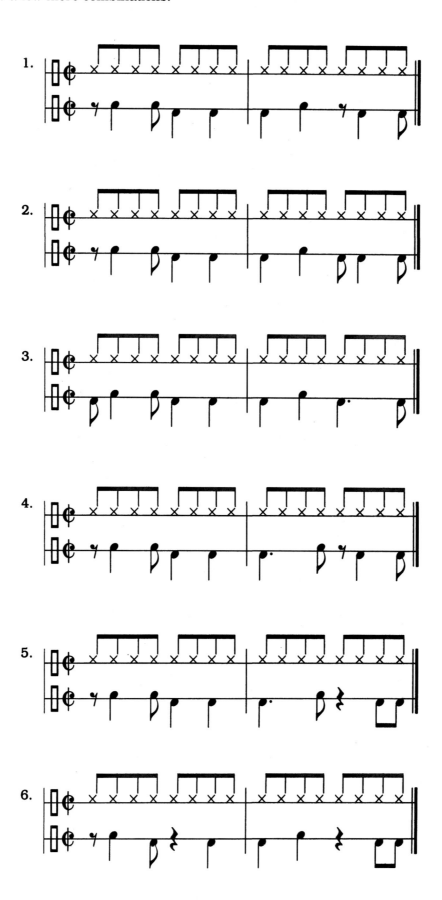

When you're comfortable with all of the patterns do the following:

1. Change the ride from the hi-hat to the cymbal and play one of the three basic ostinatos in the left foot. There are three basic rhythms you can play in your left foot:

> *Half notes (the one and two—remember you're in cut time)*
> *Offbeats (the 'ands' of one and two)*
> *Quarters (one-and two-and).*

Each will change the overall feel plus give you an added technical detail to focus on in terns of coordination. You'll go through the patterns three times; once with each of the left foot variations.

2. Go back to riding on the hi-hat. Change the right hand ride pattern. Use the ostinatos from the samba *Suggestions for Variations And Improvisation* section. Go through all of the ostinato ride variations. Each will change the feel and give you an additional technical element to address.

3. When you're comfortable with the new ride patterns put them on the ride cymbal and combine them with the three left foot (hi-hat) ostinatos. Again you'll have a new coordination element to address as well as a wealth of variations.

4. To really cover this section thoroughly you should go back and apply all of the suggestions for variations from all of the samba sections thus far.

5. Improvise and combine all of this material to develop your own variations.

Samba in 3/4

In addition to being played *in two*, there are a couple of other pulses that are quite common for the Samba. One is *three*, and the other one is *seven*, discussed in the next section. The foot pattern played in three is the same as the one for the Samba in two, but of course the one beat pattern is repeated three times. Instead of the heavier pulse being on the upbeat of the bar, as in the duple meter, the strong beat is the downbeat of each bar. Again, you have a foot ostinato and rhythmic phrases for the hands. The exact same approach should be taken here as for the other Sambas. Practice this section as follows:

1. Play all phrases on the next page with the hands in unison over the foot patterns indicated below.

2 Play the right hand on the snare and fill in the missing eighths with the left hand. (Both hands are on the snare.)

3. Do the same as number two except play the left hand on the hi-hat.

4. Play the six ostinatos from *Samba; Suggestions for Variations and Improvisation* section on the hi-hat and then the cymbals, with the following phrases in the left hand.

For additional variations and concepts for improvisation apply all of the instructions from that samba section to the rhythms written here.

Here are three foot patterns. The top line is the bass drum and the bottom the hi-hat.

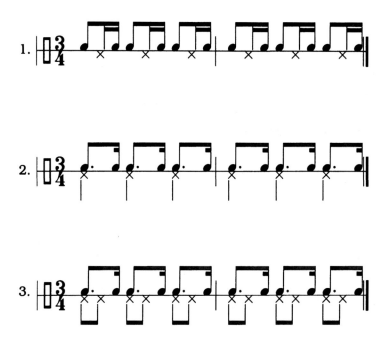

Here are some one bar phrases you can use to get started. Once you're comfortable, put them together into two bar and longer phrases.

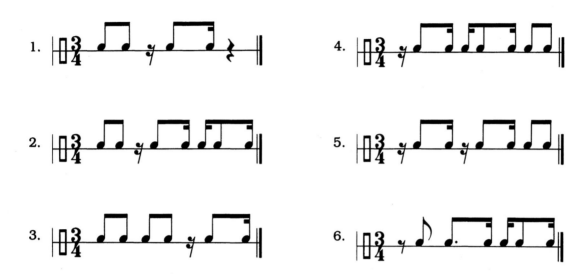

Here are some examples of two bar phrases.

By the way, if you want to hear a great Samba in 3/4 check out *Cravo y Canela* by *Milton Nascimento*. This translates into clove and cinnamon. It's been recorded quite a bit by both Brazilian and American artists.

Samba in 7/4

Samba in Seven refers to Samba where the seven beat phrase takes place twice or splits in half the length of one bar. For example: one bar of 7/4 is played as two bars of 7/8. Although the actual time signature doesn't matter, this *does not* refer to a feel where every beat gets an equal pulse. In that case you would play as if there were a full bar of 7/4, and the bass drum pattern would fit evenly into the bar—once per beat. This samba in seven is felt and played with a *one–two, one–two, one–two-three* or a *one–two, one–two, one–two and* pulse and feel. In actual playing you can almost feel this in two, but with the last beat being cut in half or dropped.

The steps for putting the whole thing together are the same as for the other Sambas. Take the phrases over the foot patterns with all the previous suggestions for variations and improvisation. The catch here is that you are sort of trying to round out the unevenness of the phrases. You don't want to make this feel jerky or disruptive of the flow of the groove. The feel needs to be smooth like the Sambas in duple meters. Following is an illustration of how this dropping of the last beat translates into the counting of the bars:

This example can be counted like this: where the counting of the word seven only gets one syllable—"sev"—,

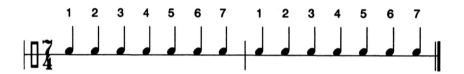

or it can get counted like this: where the counting of the word four gets no "and" syllable.

It doesn't matter how you actually count as long as you're playing the right feel.

Here are some basic foot patterns:

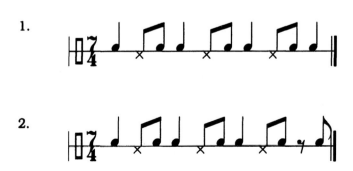

Now play the following patterns with your hands in unison on the cymbal and snare over the foot ostinatos. Then practice the rhythms in one hand with the other hand ghosting the missing notes. This is from the Samba in 2 section. Apply all of those approaches here also.

1.

2.

3.

4.

5.

6.

7.

Here are some of the previous rhythmic patterns orchestrated around the snare and toms. The center line is the snare and the high and low lines apply to the high and low toms.

1.

2.

3.

Now work with the following ostinatos as ride patterns, and play the phrases from the previous page in various ways around the kit. These ostinatos are only two beats long so they'll have to be rounded out to work in seven. Examples of this are on the next page. Another option is to play them as written and they'll round out every two bars.

1.

2.

3.

The ostinatos might get played like this when you articulate them in seven:

If you need to see both parts together to work it out, just write a hand pattern over a foot pattern. This might be especially useful when the rhythm in each hand is a little more complex as in example two. The top line is cymbal and snare and the bottom line the bass drum and hi-hat.

Significant Artists and Suggested Listening
Samba

Following is a list of composers, instrumentalists, and ensembles who made significant contributions to the development of the Samba, and are renowned for their work in this idiom. The purpose of the list is to aid in you becoming familiar with important musicians in this idiom. In building a library of this style, you can look for recordings by these artists, or with contributions from them. Many of these artists are also known for their work in other Brazilian styles as well.

Sinhô
—Early sambista from the Praça Onze area. Composer of many famous carnaval sambas.

Joaó da Baiana
—Early sambista from Praça Onze. Composer and performer. Credited with introducing the pandeiro as a samba instrument.

Donga
—Early sambista from the Praça Onze area. Co-composed the first samba, *Pelo Telefone.*

Banda Odeon
—Samba group from Praça Onze that *covered* (performed and popularized) the first samba, *Pelo Telefone.*

Pixinguinha
—Also from Praça Onze, considered one of samba's founding fathers. Arranger who introduced progressive harmony and melody to sambas. Composer of many famous sambas and leader of a group called *Os Batutas.*

Ismael Silva
—Important composer from Estaçio. Wrote many famous and influential sambas.

Nilton Bastos
—Important composer from Estaçio. Co-wrote many famous and influential sambas.

Armando Marçal
—Important composer from Estaçio. Co-wrote many famous sambas with Bide.

Bide
—Important composer from Estaçio. Part of an influential songwriting team with Armando Marçal.

Ataulfo Alves
—Singer and composer whose songs became very popular due to the emerging media of radio in the 1930's.

Assis Valente
—Singer and songwriter from Minas Gerais whose sambas also became very popular through the radio.

Moreira da Silva
—Singer and songwriter who innovated a style called *samba de breque,* in which the singer would stop and characterize the situation in the lyrics.

Ary Barroso:
—Composer of Aquarela do Brasil as well as many internationally recognized Brazilian pieces. Collaborated extensively with other composers. His compositions were recorded by many Brazilian as well as American artists.

Noel Rosa
—Guitarist with major influence in the samba cançao styles that led to the Bossa Nova.

Braguinha
—Popular songwriter of the carnaval sambas.

Dorival Caymmi
—Composer, guitarist, vocalist. Internationally renowned and innovative composer of many of the most well-known Brazilian standards.

Lamartine Babo
—Famed composer of many samba cançao standards.

Nelson Cavaquinho
—Famed cavaquinho and guitar player associated with the *samba de morro* style. Composer and innovator of an approach to the guitar.

Silas de Oliveira.
—Famed composer of many sambas de morro.

Clementina de Jesus
—Considered a living legend who recorded her first album when she was in her late sixties. She revived many obscure Brazilian pieces from many styles.

Martinho da Vila
—Well known composer and leader of famous Escolas de Samba. Innovator of approaches to the Escola's Enredos of the sixties.

Zé Keti
—Composer of many carnaval sambas. Significant figure in the samba de morro movement of the 1950's.

Paulinho de Viola
—Major samba figure and founder of the Escola de Samba *Portela*.

Famous Escolas de Samba:

—**Deixa Falar**
—**Estaçao Primeira de Mangueira**
—**Vila Isabel**
—**Arranco do Engenho Dentro**
—**Portela**
—**Quilombo**
—**Imperio Serrano**

Various other Artists

The following are great Brazilian artists whose music has been influenced by the many songstyles of Brazil. Their music is not always exclusively samba.

—**Nara Leáo**
—**Clara Nunes**
—**Beth Carvalho**
—**Elis Regina**
—**Maria Bethania**
—**Gal Costa**
—**Chico Buarque**
—**Milton Nascimento**
—**Djavan**
—**Ivan Lins**
—**Caetano Veloso**
—**Jorge Ben**
—**Gilberto Gil**
—**Toninho Orta**

Choro/Chorinho

The *Choro*—or *Chorinho*—style was born in Rio de Janeiro in the mid to late nineteenth century. It is a style that has clearly shown the influence that jazz and improvisation, as well as European harmonies and songstyles, have had on musicians in Brazil. Early Choro music was similar to the Dixieland and Rag styles that were developing in New Orleans. Both exhibited the assimilation of the African culture with improvisation. In some estimations, Choro even predated the New Orleans styles that were leading to the development of what is now our jazz. Bearing in mind how musically oriented the Brazilian culture is, this is certainly possible.

The Choro is a fast to super-fast tempo style originally featuring the flute, as lead instrument, the cavaquinho, providing rhythmic accompaniment, the guitar, often playing the bass parts, and percussion. This instrumentation has grown over time to incorporate all the instruments you would hear in an acoustic or electric jazz group. It features sophisticated harmonic progressions, modulations, and difficult melodic passages. Traditionally, the flutist would improvise melodies and the rhythm instruments would try to imitate the phrase. An improvised dialogue would develop, until the rhythm could no longer keep up with the lead. This point was called the *derrubada*, or *falling apart*. Many Choros were written specifically for the challenge of performing the song and the dare between the soloist and the other musicians. Today there are many stylized interpretations of this song form, and all continue to have the spirit of the instrumental challenge to the player.

Following are some basic patterns played for the Choro. Like all other drum set parts in this music, you are drawing from percussion parts for your patterns. Since the style is improvisational in nature, these patterns become just a framework. Think of them like a jazz groove. You can do with them whatever the music calls for and your imagination allows. Number one is for hi-hat and bass drum, number two is played on the snare. You can add two and four on the hi-hat with your left foot. Number three is a full drum set adaptation. These are only frameworks so improvise. *Also practice these patterns with the Baião bass drum pattern.* Again, since the style is improvisational and instrumental, many different variations have been derived from it and it has been interpreted in many different ways. You should approach this style like you would playing jazz. You need to be able to just play freely with a variety of rhythms and follow and interact with the improvisation.

1.

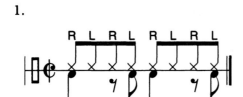

2.

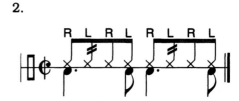

3.

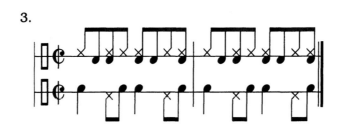

Baiaó
Introduction

The conceptual approach for the Baiaó and related styles on the drum set is much like that for the Samba. It is also a style whose patterns are basic frameworks from which you develop the feel for whatever musical situation you are in. Again, much like the approach to playing jazz—you have several types of patterns you use and the rest is improvisational. If the situation you are in is not oriented towards improvisation, then you would use more repetitive patterns and occasional variations. The material that follows should give you plenty to draw from for most situations that require these types of rhythms. Again, go back and review the percussion parts. Listen to as much of this style as possible and learn as many songs as you can. Memorize this material and then practice improvising with it to develop your own approach.

As mentioned in the *Tips for Drum Set* section, keep in mind that orchestrating your patterns on the drum set differently than you normally do can give you totally new grooves. Many times the sticking patterns remain the same. You just move them to different sound sources and the feel changes completely. This seems obvious but you'll be surprised at how many new things you will come up with by working with this. Along the same lines, you will also often keep the same rhythmic pattern but you will stick it differently. This will also give you a completely different feel and set of possibilities around the drum kit.

Baiaó Percussion Score

Here is a basic score of the traditional percussion section to refresh your memory before you start on the drum set parts. These are only basic patterns. In actual playing there can be many variations.

Baiaó
Basic Drum Set Approaches

Following are various approaches to the Baiaó rhythm. Like the other rhythms, there are basic frameworks which identify it, and *many* different ways it can be played. Get familiar with its basic patterns and a few grooves that work for you so you can function in this style. Once this is done, you can start expanding to the other approaches. It is important that you improvise to become comfortable with variations, and to expand your vocabulary.

The foundation for the Baiaó is the following pattern, which is played on the bass drum or a combination of the bass drum and the floor tom It is based on the rhythm played on the *Surdo or Zabumba*—the bass drum of the Baiaó.

As a variation the last note of the three or the first note of the three is omitted.

Variation 1:

Variation 2:

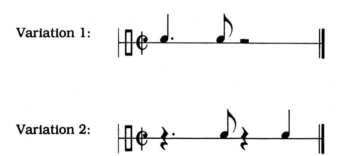

These are two very common variations to the basic patterns above. They are not played as steady patterns but as variations—the way you would play a fill or syncopation.

1.   2.

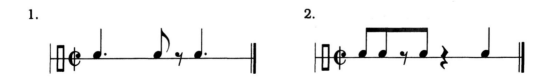

Along with the bass drum patterns on the previous page, you can play any one of the following hi-hat patterns. Combine all three of these with all of the bass drum patterns.

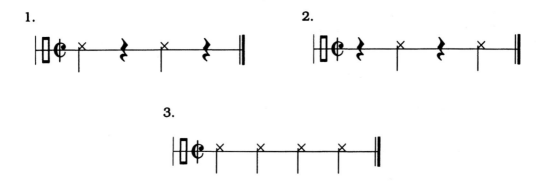

Now that you have the foot patterns down, start adding the hands. The following is a very basic time feel which works very well when there is a lot of other percussion involved because of its simplicity. *The hands are played on the hi-hat over the basic foot pattern. (You can also do this on the snare and bass drum.)* You will add embellishments in the form of accents, opening the hi-hat, buzz strokes, rolls, etc. If you can do this without any problem then move ahead. If you're not familiar or comfortable with this feel, practice the exercise that follows.

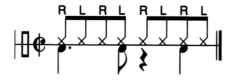

This exercise will help you get a time feel happening with the three foot patterns on the previous page foot. Take all the rhythms on the next page and practice them as follows:

1. Both hands play on the hi-hat (also do this on the snare drum). Practice the accents. You are going through accenting one eighth note at a time. Notice how each one feels and how it changes the time feel slightly.

2. Do the same as number one except open the hi-hat where the accent is written.

3. Improvise. Incorporate all kinds of embellishments.

Here is the sticking written out with the accents:

1.
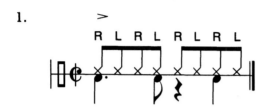

5.
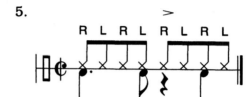

2.
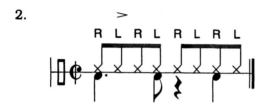

6.
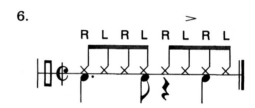

3.
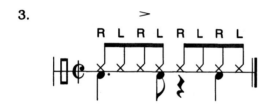

7.
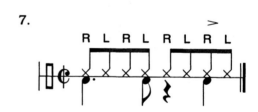

4.
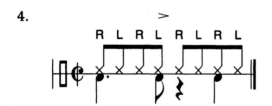

8.
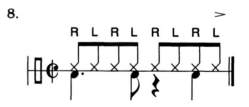

Now do this same thing on the snare and around the set. Then work with this same concept but with different stickings. For example, instead of RLRL-RLRL try using RRLR-RRLR or RRLR-RLRL. Improvise with these stickings around the set. They will each result in very different sounds and patterns.

Next, I suggest playing some phrases with the hands in unison—cymbal and snare—as was done with the first Sambas presented. This is not only for technical exercise, but is one of the ways to play the Baiaó.

Here are some phrases to start with. You should also go back and use all the two bar phrases from the Samba and Bossa Nova sections.

1.

2.

3.

4.

5.

6.

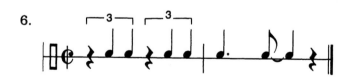

7.

Now that you've done the preliminary exercises, proceed with the following:

1. The accent variations that you practiced on the hi-hat should also be done on the snare drum. Add accents, buzz strokes, rim shots, etc.

2. Take all the two bar phrases you just played with the hands in unison over the foot patterns, and practice the *filling-in* exercise from the *Samba: Suggestions for Variations and Improvisation* section that you did with the Samba rhythms. This should give you a lot of variations. If you want more written combinations to work with, use all of the two bar Samba and Bossa Nova rhythms.

3. This is a very traditional way of playing Baião on the snare drum. It comes from the *Maxixe* rhythm.

4. Following are two very common approaches to the Baião rhythm on the drum set. The patterns involve playing an ostinato in the right hand, with a steady phrase in the left hand over the basic foot pattern. The only difference between the two is the right hand, but notice how it changes the feel.

1.

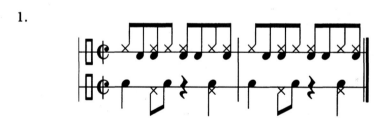

2.

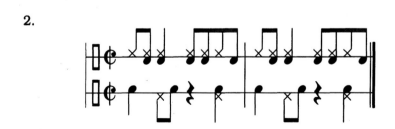

The next approach involves a thorough working of various ostinatos in the hands. Although not traditional in practice, the results give you some great grooves for this style, and it is also a great exercise for coordination and general technique.

Ostinatos will be used in the following ways:

1. Both hands playing the ostinato in unison.
2. One hand playing one ostinato and the other hand playing another ostinato simultaneously.
3. One hand playing an ostinato and the other improvising.

The final result should be that you use a combination of all the techniques—ostinatos in one or both hands, playing figures in unison, and breaking things up—so that only the music and your imagination are dictating what you play.

Following is a list of all the fifteen possible one beat combinations working from one half note to its four eighth note subdivisions. You can also do this working from one quarter note to its four sixteenth note subdivisions. The sound will be the same. Only the notation will be different.

Here is a specific approach for working with the ostinatos:

1. Play all the ostinatos with the hands in unison over all of the foot patterns. This may feel awkward at first, depending on your technical level. Just keep working on it. It will be great for your time and coordination. When you're comfortable with this start on number two.

2. Take one ostinato at a time in the right hand, and play all the other ostinatos with the left hand. When you've played all fifteen against the one in your right hand, practice improvising phrases while keeping the ostinato in your other hand. Work until you can improvise freely without changing the ostinato pattern. As a supplemental exercise, you can read rhythm lines like those in the *Modern Reading Text in 4/4* by Louis Bellson and Gil Breines, or *Syncopation* by Ted Reed.

   In the course of this exercise you will find that some rhythms feel very natural, and some feel very awkward. This may only be a technical limitation at first, but you will definitely find that some lend themselves more to the Baiaó feel than others. Those that don't feel like they work probably don't, and you should never try to force them into music; they'll probably just be a technical workout for you. This is a long term exercise. You'll get much more out of it if you're patient and take your time with it.

3. If you really want a coordination workout, take exercise number two and reverse it. That is, play the fixed ostinato with the left hand and do the workouts with the right hand.

4. Next I suggest you create *fixed patterns*—one bar in length at first, then longer phrases—by combining one ostinato in the right hand, with a different one in the left. These can be great timekeeping patterns. Although you've been practicing many ways to play variations and improvise, keep in mind that when you're playing with an ensemble, most music requires repetitive parts. Make sure you work on making all of these patterns groove. Some examples of combinations follow the rhythms on the next page.

Here are the fifteen rhythms you'll use as your ostinato patterns. *I strongly suggest you memorize these.*

1.

8.

2.

9.

3.

10.

4.

11.

5.

12.

6.

13.

7.

14.

15.

Here are some examples of two ostinato patterns put together to create a time feel. The possibilities here are endless when you use different rhythmic combinations and orchestrations. Just pick any two ostinatos to get started. Later you can combine longer phrases. Improvise.

1.

2.

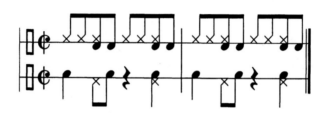

3.

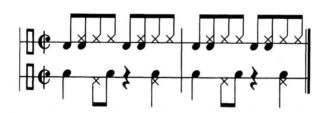

4.

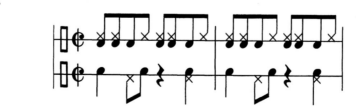

The following combinations are identical to the ones you practiced in one of the Samba sections. They here because they relate directly to the ostinato patterns you were just working on, and they make great Baiaó grooves.

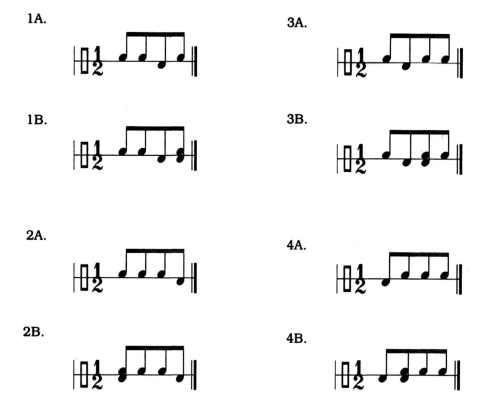

Significant Artists and Suggested Listening
Baiaó

Following is a list of artists and ensembles who made significant contributions to the development of the Baiaó and related northern styles. They are renowned for their work in these idioms. There are many styles from the north of Brazil and this list presents artists under this one broad category. Look for their names and compositions on the recordings of other artists as well.

Dorival Caymmi
—One of the most renowned and influential composers from Bahia. His songs have been performed by many of Brazil's greatest artists as well as sung by him.

Luiz Gonzaga
—Most renowned figure of Baiaó music. He was a composer, singer, accordionist and cultural figurehead from the north. Recorded the song *Baiaó* in 1946. This became the name for this new style that he practically reinvented.

Lampiáo
—Accordionist, singer and outlaw from the north. He was a hero-bandit figure who inspired Luiz Gonzaga and others.

Jackson do Pandeiro
—Singer, songwriter and percussionist. Master of two styles, *Coco* and *Embolada.*

Dominguinhos
—Accordionist, songwriter. Well-known in the style called *forro.*

Joaó do Vale
—Songwriter and singer. Although not well-known, he composed many pieces that have been recorded by famous Brazilian artists.

Filhos de Gandhi
—Afoxé group of Candomble devotees that originated around 1950. They were named after Mahatma Ghandi and were a tribute to his message of independence and non-violent resistance. The group and their music had a strong resurgence in the seventies with the renewed interest in African heritage.

Olodum
—Formed in the early eighties in Bahia, this *Bloco* can almost be called a society. It is primarily a folkloric group that has integrated many styles with the styles of Bahia. It has a pop group connected to it and an organization that sponsors forums for the awareness of African culture in Brazil.

Afros e Afoxes
—Excellent recording of a collection of Afro-Brazilian music from the northern regions.

Other artists whose music includes influences from the northern styles:
—*Margareth Meneçes*
—*Hermeto Pacsoal*
—*Naná Vasconcelos*
—*Sergio Mendes*
—*Airto Moreira*
—*Toninho Orta.*

Maracatu

The Maracatu has roots in northern Brazil; more specifically Recife, in the state of Pernambuco. It is an Afro-Brazilian processional dance performed during Carnaval in these areas. It is derived from the *Conga* or *Congada*—processional dances of African origins present in the north of Brazil. There are historical accounts that in its early incarnations it was used as ritual music played for the crowning of African kings.

Following is a score of the percussion section parts for the Maracatu. As you can see it relates very closely to the Baiaó.

Drum set adaptations of this rhythm can vary greatly. To begin with, you can use the following three bass drum patterns. They are the same ones used in the Baiaó. On the following page is a common variation. Play the hi-hat on beats two and four, one and three, or on all four quarters. Two and four is the most common.

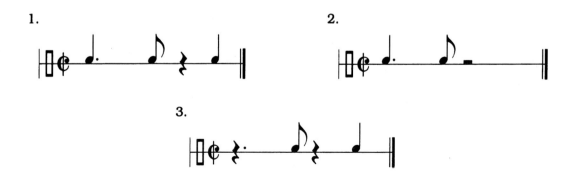

Here is another foot pattern you can use as either part of your time feel or as a variation to one of the other patterns.

This is a version of the traditional snare drum pattern. You could start your drum set feel by playing this over the foot pattern above.

Another very effective way of playing this style is to keep an ostinato with your feet, (use the Baião foot pattern), and play the following. These patterns contain the snare drum part, along with key inflections of the zabumba drum played on the toms.

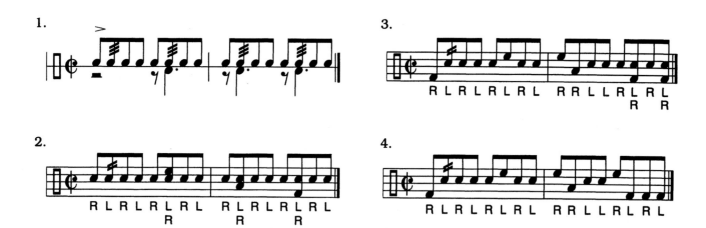

These are examples incorporating percussion parts. One hand—the top line marked "X"—is playing the ago–go bell pattern, with the other playing a condensed version of the zabumba rhythm, (or variations), on the toms or snare. The bottom system is the bass drum and hi-hat.

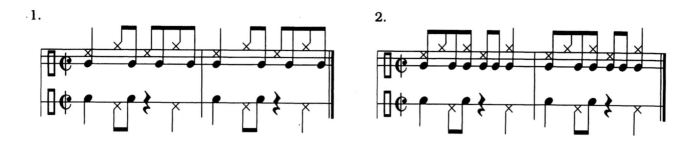

Now for a third pattern combine the first bar of each of the last two examples. This is a very typical two bar phrase.

Marcha

This *Marcha* is different from the *Samba Marcha*. Although it is also rooted, in part, in the military parade traditions, this songstyles' roots are in the northeast of Brazil. This dance and rhythm is more directly related to the Afro-Brazilian musics of the states of Bahia and Pernambuco. It is most often performed during the Carnaval festivities of these regions.

The first two examples show the rhythm of the zabumba, (or surdo/bass drum), and the pratos, (the cymbals). Play this with your bass drum and hi-hat on the drum set. The first example is the most basic pattern. The second is a common variation.

1.

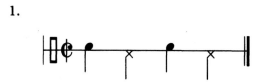

2.

The next two examples are patterns for the *caixa* (snare drum). Play these on your snare over the foot patterns notated above.

1.

2.

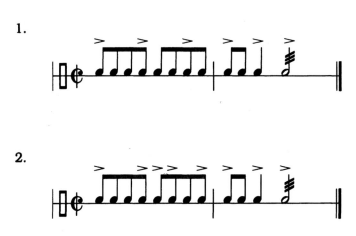

Frevo

The Frevo is a style derived from the Marcha. It is an instrumental and dance songstyle from Recife that evolved in the early 1900's. Later, in the 1970's, it was integrated with many rock styles. The name comes from the Portuguese word *ferver*, which in English means to boil. Again, it is most commonly played during Carnaval. It is a fast tempo rhythm which includes instrumental challenges for the players and whose rock instrumental interpretations sometimes border on frenzy. Although the drum set parts are relatively simple, the entire songstyle can be quite syncopated. The first example shows the bass drum and cymbals. The second and third examples show common variations you can play on the bass drum. Example four shows a full drum set part. Bass drum variations one, two, and three, can be played under the snare patterns. Examples 1a through 4a are common snare patterns. The bass drum can also double some of the accents played in the hands in patterns 1a through 4a.

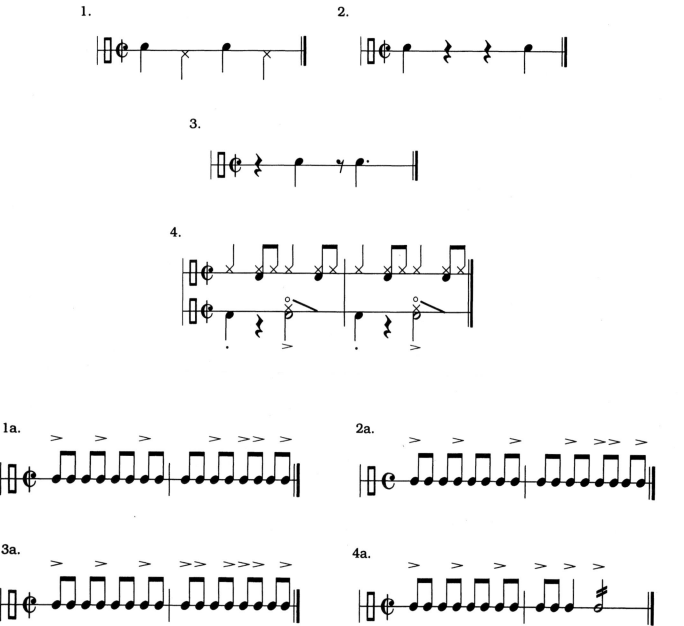

Catarete

This songstyle is derived from the Indian culture of northeastern Brazil. It is similar to the Baião—like many styles of the northeast—but evolved with a greater influence from the Indian culture, and a lesser influence from the African culture—the opposite of most other music from this region. The biggest difference on drum set is in the bass drum pattern.

This is a drum set pattern for the Catarete.

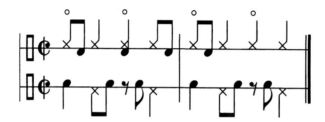

When you are comfortable with the drum set pattern, you can substitute the following rhythms for your ride pattern.

1.   2.   3.

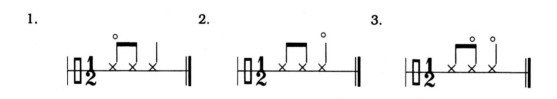

4.   5.

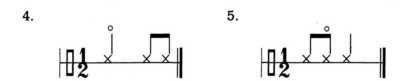

Afoxé

This is another rhythm from Bahia and the general northeastern region. The large west-African population of this region heavily influenced this songstyle. The *Afoxé* has many rhythmic variations and derivations. Its roots are in the ritual music of Candomble, which is derived from the Yoruba culture in Brazil. Yoruba stems from the Nigerian culture. It is mainly performed by *Blocos Afros*—groups of mostly black or mulato musicians who deal primarily with the African culture of Brazilian music. The traditional instruments of Afoxé are the three *Atabaque*—the *rum, rumpi* and *le*—the *gonguê*—a low pitched ago-go bell, and various *ganza*—shakers.

Following are two patterns you can use to play this rhythm on the drum set. You can also use the foot patterns from the Baião for this rhythm.

1.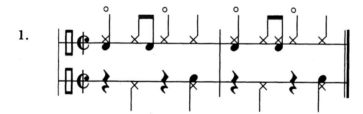

2.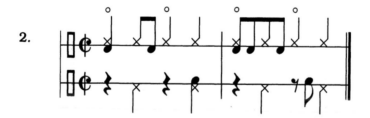

3.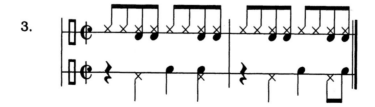

Glossary

The definitions here are presented in the context of the musical styles referred to in this book and may not necessarily be the complete or only definition of the term.

Afoxé (style)
—A songstyle and rhythm derived from the ritual music of Candomble (the Yoruban tribes and religion of Nigeria) played mainly during Carnaval in Salvador, Bahia.

Afoxé (instrument)
–A gourd wrapped with beads that are strung on chords.

Ago-gó
–A number of different size bells, (usually two), welded together by a flexible metal rod. Of African origin. Very common in Carnaval songstyles.

Apito
–A whistle. More indigenously, a Samba whistle played by the bateria's director in an Escola de Samba to cue the sections of the performance.

Atabaque
–The conga drum indigenous to Candomblé music. Name of the conga drum in Brazil.

Bahia
–State in northeastern Brazil with a large African population. Area where African musical influence is most prevalent.

Baião
–The musical songstyle of Bahia. Containing much African influence, it is characterized by its Zabumba rhythm, triangle and various harmonic and melodic characteristics.

Baixo
–Bass (guitar).

Baqueta
–Drumstick.

Bateria
–The percussion section of the Escola de Samba. A drum set.

Batucada
–A Samba played with only percussion. A percussion jam.

Berimbau
–The key instrument that accompanies Capoeira music. It is a wooden bow with a metal string and a gourd used as a resonator. It is played with a stick (that strikes rhythms on the string), caxixi (which are shaken, also for rhythm), and a coin held against the metal string (used to vibrate the string and create the unique sound on the instrument).

Bombo
–The Brazilian bass drum. (The largest of the bass drums.)

Bossa Nova
–The style of music which developed in the late 1950's in Rio de Janeiro. It included some elements of the Samba, but introduced a unique, subtle vocal style and a new rhythmic style on the acoustic guitar. The harmonies were influenced by both European and jazz musics.

Caixa
–Snare drum.

Caixeta
–Wood block or temple block.

Candomble
–Afro-Brazilian religion derived from the Yoruba (West African/Nigerian) culture. Practiced mostly in Bahia. It incorporates the Atabaque drums (Brazilian conga drums).

Capoeira
–Dance and Martial-Art form of African descent, (from the Bantu culture of Angola), practiced in the north of Brazil. It is accompanied by the Berimbau.

Carioca
–Term used to describe a person or an object from Rio de Janeiro.

Carnaval
–Originally a religious (roman catholic), celebration taking place on the four days prior to Ash Wednesday (which marks the beginning of Lent, a period of fasting and abstinence). The American version would be Mardi Gras.

Catereté
–Instrumental and dance songstyle derived from the Indian culture of northern Brazil. Traditional dance accompaniment is two violins.

Cavaquinho
 –Small four-stringed guitar commonly used in Samba. Similar to a ukelele. Strings tuned to D-G-B-D.

Caxixi
 –Small weaved baskets filled with beads or pebbles. Used as a shaker along with the Berimbau in Capoeira music.

Chocalo
 –Metal (sometimes wood) canister shakers usually filled with beads or pebbles or sand.

Choro
 –Instrumental style developed in Rio in the late 1800's featuring fast tempos, challenging melodic and harmonic passages and improvisation.

Coco
 –Instrumental and dance songstyle from the northeast.

Congada
 –African and Afro-Brazilian processional dances.

Cuica
 –Also called lion's roar or friction drum. Metal or wood canister with a thin post attached to a drum skin. Produces a groaning or squeaking sound. Also used to mimic high pitched sounds of the human voice.

Entrudo
 –Early form of carnival brought to Brazil by the Portuguese which involved a riotous approach to the celebration.

Escola de Samba
 –Organization or musical society that parades in carnaval as well as sponsoring other social events in the community it's from.

Favela
 –Run down or slum neighborhood.

Forró
 –Term sometimes used to describe a dance where northeastern styles such as Baiaó are played. Generic term sometimes used to describe the styles themselves.

Frevo
 –Instrumental and dance songstyle from Recife; derived from the Marcha.

Fricote
 –Songstyle that is a mixture of reggae and Afro-Brazilian styles from the north.

Frigideira
 –Percussion instrument made of frying pans welded together and played with a stick. Functions like the ago-go bells.

Ganzá
 –Weaved basket shakers filled with beads.

Habanera
 –Cuban songstyle that had an influence on the development of some Samba as well as other Brazilian styles.

Ijexá
 –Afro-Brazilian rhythm with roots in the Yoruban culture. Usually associated with the Afoxé.

Jongo
 –Type of Samba from the southern parts of Brazil.

Lambada
 –Songstyle and dance style that combines various rhythms from Brazil and the Caribbean.

Lundu
 –Songstyle brought to Brazil by the Bantu slaves from Angola. Influenced the early developments of various Brazilian styles.

Maracatu
 –Processional song and dance style derived from the *congada*. Developed in Recife and neighboring regions.

Marcha
 –Song and dance style of northern Brazil. Early developments were influenced by some European and American two-beat dance styles.

Marcha-Rancho
 –Slower version of the Marcha with more focus on the song's melody.

Maxixe
 –Brazilian songstyle and dance developed in the late 1800's. It was a combination of various European ballroom dance styles as well as the polka, tango, Cuban habanera and the African lundu.

Mestre-Sala
 –Master of ceremonies of the Escola de Samba. Marches around the *Porta-Bandeira* (flag-bearer) in the Escola's parade.

Mestre-de Bateria
 –The leader of the percussion section of the Escola de Samba. Often the musical conductor for the entire ensemble.

Morro

–As in *Samba de Morro* (Samba of the hills). Describes the hills around Rio where most of the *favelas* are located and where most of the developments of Samba took place.

Orixá

–A deity of many Afro-Brazilian religions.

Pandeiro

–The Brazilian tambourine.

Partido Alto

–Type of Samba with a call and response vocal style and a unique rhythm that was an offshoot for many Brazilian-Funk feels.

Passista

–The Samba dancers of the Escola.

Porta-Bandeira

–The flag-bearer of the Escola de Samba.

Pratos

–Cymbals. Usually a hand-held pair used in some Escolas.

Reco-reco

–Instrument made from metal or bamboo with ridges. Today it is metal with springs stretched across its length. It is scraped with a stick and produces the sound of a scratcher. Most often used by Escolas in Carnaval.

Repinique, (repique)

–Two-headed, high-pitched drum used in Escolas de Samba to give cues to the ensemble. Also used as a solo feature in various contemporary Brazilian styles.

Samba

–The most famous (along with Bossa Nova) and influential Brazilian instrumental and dance-style. Most common in duple meter with vocal choruses and syncopated orchestration.

Samba-Cancaó

–Samba form developed in the early 1900's by the middle and upper class musicians featuring the lyrics and a more subdued instrumental approach.

Samba enredo

–The enredo is the *theme-samba* played by an Escola during carnaval.

Surdo

–The bass drum of the Samba. Comes in three sizes. Played with a mallet and the hand.

Tamborim

–Small tambourine-shaped instrument. Played with a stick (sometimes multi-pronged) and the hand.

Xaxado

–Songstyle from the northeast. Predecessor to the Baiaó styles.

Yoruba

–An African culture from Nigeria whose music had great influence on the development of Brazilian music.

Zabumba

–A bass drum used in the Baiaó and other styles from the north of Brazil.